SCHOOL X

JETHRO JONES

How principals can design a transformative school experience
for students, teachers, parents – and themselves

First published 2020

by John Catt Educational Ltd,
15 Riduna Park, Station Road
Melton, Woodbridge IP12 1QT

Tel: +44 (0) 1394 389850
Fax: +44 (0) 1394 386893
Email: enquiries@johncatt.com
Website: www.johncatt.com

ISBN: 978 1 91362 211 4

Set and designed by John Catt Educational Limited

Reviews

Actionable, urgent insights for any principal ready to re-engage in the work that brought them to the field in the first place.

Seth Godin, author, *Stop Stealing Dreams*

The evidence is clear. The learning experiences happening at a school are highly correlated with the effectiveness of the school's principal. In *SchoolX*, Jethro Jones outlines a highly impactful, human-centered design model to support principals in becoming the leader they want to be, and the role model their students and staff so desperately need.

Thomas C. Murray, director of innovation,
Future Ready Schools, Washington, D.C.

The phrase "school transformation" has never felt more attainable. Jones has done something I have not seen before: he's illuminated the link between design thinking and principalship in ridiculously helpful terms. *SchoolX* is the path to improving how all stakeholders experience your school.

Dr. Brad Gustafson, award-winning principal and author

Jones is a voracious reader and he is learning how to take lessons he's learned and apply them to helping others lead more effectively. This book supports those who want to design better learning environments for all and has loads of strategies and skills to do so effectively.

Jennifer Abrams, communications consultant

SchoolX is full of practical and actionable insight into the ecosystem of a school from the perspective of all stakeholders. Jones takes you on a transformational journey through relatable stories, research-based practices, and design thinking to make meaningful and intentional changes. He does all of this through a humble exploration of how change might be made in relation to each stakeholder. *SchoolX* is a fantastic tool to help you reimagine school through deliberate design.

Kelly Tenkely, executive director and principal

As a veteran classroom teacher, I appreciate Jones' all-encompassed focus on the teacher, student, and parent experience taking place each day inside the classroom. His work gracefully weaves theory and practice, equipping school leaders with tangible next steps to enhance the school experience for all stakeholders.

Mitch Weathers, founder, Organized Binder, Inc.

The job of a principal is constantly changing and the pressures are evolving. *SchoolX* takes you through practical ways to transform any school to make it better for students, parents, and the community. Jones has examined many different facets of leadership and the transformation process, while explaining them to the readers so they can implement tomorrow. *SchoolX* will help new and seasoned leaders grow exponentially.

Ryan Sheehy, educator/author/speaker

Jones masterfully frames the school experience from multiple perspectives and provides valuable suggestions on how to collectively transform schools. Now, more than ever, we need innovative school leaders that have the capacity to listen, learn, and lead real change in our schools. *SchoolX* is the perfect guide to achieve those goals in a holistic approach to school improvement.

Dr. Greg Goins, director of educational leadership at Georgetown College, Kentucky, and host of the *Reimagine Schools* podcast

Jones takes the reader through the experiences of school leaders, teachers, students, and families. I found it illuminating that he focused on the "experiences" of each group, as it is our experiences that make up our point of view and shape our approach to education. In each section, he demonstrates ways for educators to transform from managers and leaders to designers, with the focus always remaining on our students. Drawing on his own experiences as well as nuggets of wisdom from educators across the country (many of whom are inspirations to me as well), Jones provides a vision for educational leadership and practical steps to turn the vision into a reality.

Jonathon Wennstrom, elementary principal, Michigan

SchoolX is a must-read for every school principal! Jones does an amazing job of presenting rich and effective ideas that are based on research and from savvy leaders.

Thomas R. Hoerr, scholar in residence, University of Missouri-St. Louis

Schools make up the fiber of a community. Students, parents, teachers, and the community either feel pride in their schools or they don't. So much of it is about the daily experiences people have from the minute they enter the building, to the emotions people carry when they leave the school building. *SchoolX* is an essential guide for anyone who wants to be part of an organization that embodies learning.

Anthony Kim, author and entrepreneur

Principals now more than ever need to think about how to redesign traditional schools for the benefit of their students, faculty and parents. Jones curates thoughtful insights from leading educational experts and identifies the key strategies that you can implement to transform the culture of your school. *SchoolX* is a need-to-read book to help elevate your school to new heights.

Winston Y. Sakurai, NASSP Digital Principal of the Year 2016

SchoolX is a book that will help transform education and leadership as we know it. Jones provides great examples throughout the book on how to create learning environments seen through the eyes of our students, teachers, and parents. *SchoolX* does a great job explaining the different nuances of leadership, including the importance of intangibles and how extremely important the student experience is in changing education. There are opportunities throughout the book allowing the reader to reflect on his or her current practices. It is also packed with ideas and easy-to-follow steps to assist leaders. It really is a one-stop shop for educational leadership. This book is a must-read for everyone in a leadership position who wants to change the traditional school experience and help the future of education.

Bobby Dodd, principal, Mason High School, Ohio

This hands-on and actionable book is bound together with many real-world examples and practical advice from numerous experts in the field of education. Jones' writing style helps you feel more like you are sitting down with him in your local coffee shop than you are turning pages in a book.

Jon Harper, assistant principal

Contents

Introduction

The role of school principal may be one of the most unique positions in any organization. There aren't many other roles that require a leader to interface with so many stakeholders, with such drastic and diverse expectations for success in different areas. The expectations from one stakeholder group often completely oppose the expectations from another group. For example, teachers want higher pay and lower class sizes, but the community wants lower taxes, and the district wants a recent school board initiative followed through on, while the state legislature (hypothetically) has mandated that all classrooms have at least two standing desks for students. And, no, they didn't allocate extra money for this.

What is the school experience?
The school experience (SchoolX) is how the school is experienced by anyone who interacts with it. It is imperative for school leaders to think about what all stakeholders experience, but it may be a challenge for you to find the time to do all the things we will talk about in this book. If you are stuck in what the leadership guru Chris LoCurto calls the "leadership crazy cycle", you won't have the time to do anything!

If you feel like you're in a crazy cycle, I would encourage you to go to part 1 and establish your mission and vision, to make sure your time spent is worthwhile and meaningful. And remember, you're not alone!

The design-thinking process
You're reading this book because you want to be a designer – you want to design your school to meet the needs of the people there. We are going to

discuss a lot of the problems that you face every day as a principal, so let's define the process by which you, as a designer, will solve those problems.

The design-thinking process is a problem-solving process. It all hinges around the idea of attempting to solve problems quickly and efficiently (but not necessarily perfectly). When you examine the experiences of your stakeholders, anything that you need to change will be considered a "problem".

Below is a chart describing the design-thinking process. I also refer you to my interview with Susie Wise from Stanford's d.school (also known as the Hasso Plattner Institute of Design) to learn more about how it applies to education, specifically. You can find the interview on my website: schoolx.me/susie

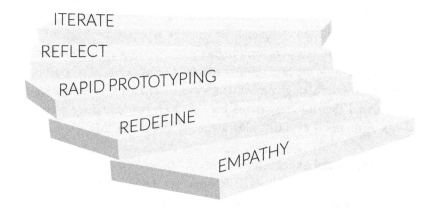

ITERATE
REFLECT
RAPID PROTOTYPING
REDEFINE
EMPATHY

The first step in the process is to gain **empathy**, in a human-centered way. When a stakeholder interacts with the school in a way that decreases the enjoyment or quality of their experience, you need to find out how they feel about that. Saying, "I think they feel this way" isn't good enough. You must *feel* what it is like to be in their shoes. I'll weave in a specific story to teach the ideas in a broad sense. In my school, we had a small cafeteria and 200 kids at lunch. People kept telling me that we needed a third lunch sitting because it took kids too long to get their meals. But we needed to feel what the kids were feeling to figure out why lunch was taking so long.

When you gain empathy, you are seeking trouble spots or pain points. You are looking for things that aren't contributing to a positive school experience for that person (Susie Wise created the #shadowastudent movement, which involves principals and teachers experiencing what a school day is like for students).

Once you have empathy, **redefine the problem**. It's important to gain empathy first, because you may not really know what the problem is, or the problem may be disguised on the surface. Sometimes you may spot a problem, but before you can define what it is, you must gain empathy to uncover the issues behind it. At my school, we knew there was a problem with lunch, but we had to gain empathy to figure out *why* the problem existed, and only then could we define the problem accurately.

After empathy and defining the problem, it's time to think about some solutions. The solutions are much better when you know what the actual problem is, so don't skip the step of gaining empathy. We thought our problem was that we had too many kids in the cafeteria at once, so we needed either a third lunch sitting or a longer lunch. When we had empathy, though, we found that the real problem was that the line moved too slowly.

The next step is **rapid prototyping**. Once you have a prototype for the solution to the problem, you try it out. Our prototype solution was to make the kids get in line first, not sit down. The challenge with prototyping is that education is typically very slow in any kind of change. This is where it is awesome to be a school principal, because you can make an immediate change and see if it works.

The next step is to **reflect**. What went well or didn't go well? Did the problem get solved? If it didn't, we were wrong in our first prototype. So, we **iterate**. We change our focus and see if we can solve the problem with our next prototype.

Now let's delve a little deeper into the design-thinking process.

Empathy

To start with empathy is to build an understanding of what a stakeholder feels and experiences. Gaining their perspective is vital. You can gain perspective in many ways, all of which involve action.

Let's look at this a little more closely. In my school, we noticed that the cafeteria staff were cleaning up lunch before all the kids were served. To gain perspective, we asked the cafeteria staff what they thought was happening. They said that they started cleaning up when the line ended. To gain empathy, we asked the kids why they didn't get lunch. We found out that they didn't want to wait in line, so were sitting down with their friends until the line was shorter. But they got distracted talking with their friends and took too long to get in line, and the cafeteria staff were so efficient that they saw no more kids in line and got to work cleaning up.

> **Empathy-gaining strategies**
> - Surveys.
> - Shadow a student (or teacher, parent, community member).
> - Go through the process yourself.
> - Just talk to people.

After you gain empathy, you need to go deeper. We knew the line moved fairly quickly and the cafeteria staff had many of the lunches prepped and ready to go. So we spent an afternoon in the cafeteria monitoring the situation, and saw that it took about 45 seconds from the time kids got their lunch to the time they were able to leave the lunch line. This doesn't seem like that long, but all that is left after getting your lunch is entering your number in the computer.

Through gaining empathy, we had identified the problem. We defined it as this: how do we get the kids their lunch fast enough that they don't mind waiting in line?

Rapid-prototype

In this key part of the design-thinking process, you need to rapid-prototype. This stage is not about getting everyone onboard; it is about simple, forward-thinking steps in the right direction. We're not talking about school-wide initiatives that will be big changes, although this process also works for those larger initiatives. What we are focusing on here is ensuring that we are making incremental improvements to the experience.

Our first prototype in solving our cafeteria problem was to not let the kids sit down until they had their lunch. We made this decision based on the perspective of the cafeteria staff. But the students didn't like this prototype solution and it quickly turned into a nightmare to manage kids who were not getting their food fast enough and were standing in line for too long. The result was annoyed and hungry kids.

Reflect

After we prototype, we need to see if we have solved the problem. Sometimes, we solve problems that we didn't know we had. Other times, we create new problems with our solution. Neither of these are bad. The idea here is to continue to improve.

Our first prototype didn't solve our lunch problem. So, after reflecting on the experience of the kids, we installed a second computer for collecting their lunch numbers. What we saw was a reduction to 11 seconds per student to get their food. That was significantly better than 45 seconds! And guess what happened? The kids stopped waiting for the line to go down before getting their lunches. They knew they wouldn't have to wait long for their food. With this prototype, the last of the 200 kids had food and was sitting down after just 10 minutes.

Iterate

When we reflected further, we realized that there were still things we could do better. We now have an aide stationed at the computers to make sure the right kids get credited with the food purchase, ensure we meet federal regulations, and assist if there are any issues. Initially, the aide was just looking on, waiting for the kids to enter their numbers, but we found we could streamline the system even more by having the aide enter the numbers for the kids, so they can get through even faster. This important additional change removed all bottlenecks from the system. Now, students get their food and, most of the time, go right to their seat after receiving a smile from the aide assisting them.

Why go through this process?

When you go out of your way to make the experience better for students, they understand that you are there for *them*. Kids often feel invisible in the adult world, and even though schools are about kids, they are run by adults. That makes it difficult for students to know how to improve their own experience. Many schools are making great efforts to include kids in the process of making the school better, but many students still feel like there is nothing they can do to change their situation in their school.

As we will see, making a school focused on kids is important, but changes need to happen in order for our schools to truly focus on students.

The leadership experience

Didn't I just say that schools need to be focused on students? Shouldn't I focus on the student experience, first?

Sadly, no.

As a school principal, can you make a significant change to the student experience if you are constantly running around putting out fires? Can you seek empathy if you are constantly running from one emergency to the next? You can't. Chris LoCurto calls this the "leadership crazy cycle". But it doesn't have to be crazy. We will delve more into how to solve the leadership crazy cycle in part 1, but I want to touch on it here.

There are two major roles that a principal fills in schools: manager and instructional leader. We'll save the roles of mediator, confidant, coach, supporter, nurse, and so many more for later. The work that is in your job description is really about being a manager or an instructional leader.

In order to improve the student experience, you need to improve your own experience first. This means carving out time for tasks that are important and urgent, and delegating the things that aren't (the Eisenhower matrix is a useful tool for this; see page 32).

Two key ways of getting out of the leadership crazy cycle are learning to say no and scheduling your time, thus gaining control over your managerial duties. Here are a few things you can do to achieve this.

1. Define what is an emergency and what can wait. This is a challenge, because many days seem like they are full of emergencies.
2. Block out time on your calendar for specific tasks and ensure this is respected by your secretary and staff. Include classroom observations in your blocked-out time.
3. Prioritize kids being in class. When kids are sent to the principal's office, they are missing out on class. I have found success in dealing

with this by having students who come to the office put their issues down on paper. This gives the principal something to refer to, in order to see if the issue is urgent or not.

The second part of being a principal is instructional leadership. In order for you to be an effective instructional leader, you have to find ways to make sure your managerial duties do not overshadow your instructional duties. To improve your experience as an instructional leader, you need to:

1. Be in classrooms!
2. Pay attention to best practices in instruction.
3. Improve your ability to coach teachers effectively.
4. Provide opportunities for teachers to learn from each other.

If you are stuck in the leadership crazy cycle, you won't be able to focus on these priorities. And if you're going to improve anyone else's experience, your school experience cannot be that of the crazy cycle. Here are some questions to help you consider your experience as a leader.

- Do you have the time you need to make effective plans?
- Do you enjoy coming to work?
- Do you have time to work *on* your school instead of just *in* your school?
- Do you have time to accomplish all the tasks that are before you?
- Can you make timely decisions where you are not rushed or pressured into a choice?
- Do you work more than 40 hours a week, not including supervision?

The teacher experience
Teachers need support! Plain and simple. Their workload is ever-increasing and a study has shown that the teacher experience is leading to 44% of new teachers quitting within the first five years.[1]

---

1 Madeline Will, "5 Things to Know About Today's Teaching Force," *Education Week*, 2018, tinyurl.com/y3zcglc7

Teachers are overburdened with rising class sizes, slashed budgets, unfunded mandates, and standardized testing. But the main reason why teachers need support is that they are human beings. Everybody needs support to be more successful. (An aside about support: supporting someone doesn't mean you give them whatever they want; it means you give them what they *need*.)

The educator and author Jeff Zoul has talked to me about how there are more bullying incidents among students in schools where teacher are bullies, and we can extrapolate that to suggest that there are teacher bullies where there are principal bullies. People often joke that leaders are on the "dark side." This phrase always annoys me, because it sets up the adversarial relationship from the word go and we don't need that in education. We are on the same team.

What the teacher experience means is that a teacher comes to work where she is appreciated, respected, and given the opportunity to do the things necessary to help kids achieve at high levels in all areas of their development.

At Chris LoCurto's Next-Level Leadership LIVE Event 2017, I heard that many employees leave their profession because of their leaders. With so many teachers quitting education, school leaders must take a hard look at themselves and see where they can improve. One of the most beneficial things we can do is to gain insight into the personalities of the teachers in our buildings, and then communicate with them in a way that will help them to be the best they can be. The type of personality test doesn't matter. What matters is having a framework for talking about these issues. I like using the DISC test because it focuses on communication, which I believe to be at the center of nearly every problem we have as humans.

It is vitally important for you to know your own personality profile, in order to be self-aware, but it is incumbent on you to also train your staff and students to be self-aware. You do this by knowing their personalities and adapting yourself to meet their needs.

The student experience

Schools are not designed for kids. There, I said it. They are designed for adults. There are so many things that get in the way of schools being for kids: negotiated agreements, board policies, bell schedules, curriculums, grades that are used to control students, and so much more. When parents ask kids what they learned at school that day, they typically respond, "Nothing." Sadly, this is not far from the truth. Many schools are not focused on what kids are learning, but instead on how compliant they are.

Rather than focusing on what is good for adults, today's school leaders need to gain empathy for students and figure out what works for *them*. Often, what works for kids is harder to enact than what works for adults. The factory model of education was great when we needed factory workers, but our kids' futures will be more different from this than we can possibly imagine.

In the spring of 2020, the coronavirus pandemic closed schools all over the world. The factory model of education that was based on the "sage on the stage" standing in front of 30 kids was no longer possible. Suddenly, students, teachers, and parents were all working and learning from home. The system was completely unprepared for this change, which was immediate and revolutionary. Educators reacted quickly and did their best to support students. Most importantly, millions of children *still learned.*

Back in school, we need to take the time to actually listen to students and *hear* what they are saying. It is possible. There are leaders out there who are connecting with their students in a powerful way and making school more meaningful for them. I talk about a few of these leaders in part 1.

Many buzzwords exist around this topic: standards-based grading, personalized learning, Genius Hour, 20% time, growth mindset, grit, perseverance, co-teaching, and many more. These need to be more than buzzwords. We need these ideas to be the basis for how we teach our students. The skills our students require to be successful are much more aligned with soft skills than they are with the curriculum maps put out by your curriculum department.

I invite you to truly listen and find out what the kids in your school need. Not what the Department of Education, or state commissioner, or even your local school board says they need. Listen to your students – and adapt.

The parent and community experience

Want to know how to really distance yourself from the people in your community? Judge them. They don't even need to hear you say anything bad about them. Judging your parents and community creates a divide between you and them that can rarely be bridged.

Your community needs communication. Don't give up on that. Focus and make sure your message is getting out in a multitude of ways. Be on all the social media you can handle and send out as much information as possible. Spend a lot of time celebrating the great things you do. Joe Sanfelippo, superintendent in Fall Creek, Wisconsin, has created a movement around #gocrickets. In fact, in Fairbanks, Alaska, I am wearing a "Go Crickets!" shirt while typing this. I couldn't be much farther from Fall Creek, but Sanfelippo's branding has reached all the way up here and had an impact on me. Do we all need to be like him? No. But our communities deserve to hear about the great things that are happening in our schools every day. And it has to be about more than just sports. If it is only sports, we are promoting a very small segment of our school.

Think about what it looks and feels like to enter your school from a parent or community perspective. One door signifies that "all are welcome," while the other door lists all the things you can't do in the school. I'm sure risk management was involved in that decision. Somewhere, in a room far away from any school, someone said, "We need to make sure that people know drugs aren't allowed in our school. I know, let's make sure that nobody within 50ft of the building can misunderstand that by plastering it all over every entrance."

Is that really necessary? Probably not. Let's make sure that school is a welcoming and inviting place for parents and the wider community.

Designing a better experience

There are three types of school leader:

1. **Managers**. They try to make sure nothing breaks and spend their time putting out fires.
2. **Leaders**. They seek to have a vision and lead the school to achieve that vision. They try to solve problems before they exist.

3. **Designers**. They try to break things that aren't working, regardless of who those things are not working for. They design their school to meet the needs of the stakeholders.

I want to show you how to create and adapt your school according to the needs of your school community; to show you how to become a *designer*, not just a manager or a leader. This book will help you to design a transformative school experience for the teacher, the student, the parent/community, and the leader. That's you! Because if you improve your own experience, then you will be able to radically transform the experiences of others.

Much of the research for this book came from my *Transformative Principal* podcast and the Transformative Leadership Summit: School Experience. The Transformative Leadership Summit is an online learning conference designed to explore and expand ideas about what is possible in education. In the Transformative Leadership Summit: School Experience, Danny Bauer and I interviewed more than 30 specialists to figure out how to improve the school experience. Many of the illuminating quotes that you will read in this book came out of those interviews.

PART 1
The leadership experience

"Now that you're all standing, you need to order yourself by your proficiency with social media." The presenter wanted me and the other leaders in the room to learn from each other about how to use social media in schools. I saw my assistant principal check his phone. He sent the calls to voicemail. He and I had been working to be more "in the moment" and had agreed to not let ourselves be interrupted all the time. It wasn't often that we were both able to be out of school attending a conference; this was a great opportunity for us to build on our leadership skills together.

As we lined up and the presenter asked us to pair the most proficient with the least proficient, my AP mouthed "social worker" to me. Almost on cue, our school's social worker called me, after being sent to the AP's voicemail. I ducked out to answer the call. Interrupting a conference session on social media use for schools wasn't the end of the world. But when I answered, she said, "Is the AP with you? I'm going to need you both." I gave my AP the eye and he followed me out of the room. Our school-based mental health clinician waited for us to find a private room and told us the story.

A student that we had all been working with was experiencing suicidal ideation. We needed to come up with a solution to the immediate crisis, and it couldn't wait. We reviewed possible interventions, considered parental support and history, and eventually decided it was appropriate to get the student to the local hospital for a suicide assessment.

As we headed back into the conference room, the presenter was finishing up the 15-minute activity we had just missed. We tried to get back into the swing of things, but the thought of that student struggling did a fair job of distracting us. When we got the thumbs-up emoji from the clinician in a group text chat, we knew the student was safe and had the support needed to avert a tragedy.

As a principal, you never know what is going to happen each day you go to school – or attend a conference. Your role is so much more than instructional leadership. Not to downplay the role of instructional leader, but that student experiencing suicidal ideation didn't need an instructional leader in her corner. She needed a compassionate, dedicated-to-her leader, who was ready to make a call that ultimately saved her life. To be successful in moments like these, you must be ready, able, and willing to switch gears, and to make a good decision in what can be a limited amount of time.

In the blank space below, tally the number of times you were interrupted or your plans were derailed in the last five school days you can remember. (It might be easier, depending on your situation, to tally the number of times your plans were *not* interrupted.)

I'm serious. Are there tally marks above this sentence? If not, go make some tally marks. Take some time to think about this.

Now that you've done that, think about those interruptions and how you felt about them. Choose two interruptions to focus on for this thought exercise. Was the school experience better for someone because you were interrupted? Would waiting have been better? Do you think you have made a meaningful impact because of that interruption?

Write your reflections here:

Your mission

Near Sitka, Alaska, there is a congruence of large rivers and inlets where the Pacific Ocean meets the land, called the Chatham Strait. In this part of the Alexander Archipelago, the waterways are always challenging to navigate, whether you are in a small kayak or a large ferry boat. Preparation and a strong constitution are required. Even on the calmest days, the treacherous waters cannot be still. These waters are similar to what a principal navigates every single day.

The secret to not getting seasick, Sitka's superintendent Mary Wegner told me, is to focus on the calm water at the end of the strait. The calm water is the mission.

We talk about mission in schools quite frequently. We spend long committee meetings planning and describing what a school or district mission statement should be. We usually get something like this:

> *"The Kodiak Island Borough School District, in close cooperation with our diverse island community, exists to provide an educational program of the highest standard that empowers all students to achieve personal and academic excellence while developing their full potential as responsible, productive citizens."*

Or something like this:

"Our mission is to provide an excellent, equitable education in a safe, supportive environment so all students will succeed and contribute to a diverse and changing society" (Fairbanks North Star Borough School District)

Or this:

"The School District of Fall Creek, along with the community, through meaningful personal connections, will provide a safe, supportive environment that inspires students to reach their academic and personal potential and to become responsible citizens."

When it comes to getting people onboard with a mission, the buzzword-focused school district has a better chance of nobody ever knowing the mission than actually achieving it. Contrast this with the following mission statements:

- "Engaged in learning, prepared for life."
- "Community that works, learns and succeeds together."
- "What is needed, when it's needed."

It doesn't matter where I teach or lead, my personal mission statement for education as it relates to staff, students, and parents is "What is needed, when it's needed." Does that mean I'm perfect and nail this all the time? No. I'm not perfect and never will be. But everything I do is focused on this core mission statement. I do what my people need, when they need it.

What is lacking from the jargon-filled mission statements is clarity and simplicity. These statements are worked on for months (if not years) and then never revised or updated. With all that work, a mission statement should stand the test of time. All it stands is the test of bureaucracy!

Contrast this with the mission statement of Lindsay Unified School District in Central Valley, California. Nik Namba of LUSD says in a podcast interview[2] that the statement was developed more than 10 years

---

2   "iNACOL with Nik Namba of Lindsay Unified School District" (podcast interview), *Personalized Learning with Matt & Courtney*, 2017, tinyurl.com/vc72jda

THE LEADERSHIP EXPERIENCE

ago and still guides every decision made in that district: "Empowering and motivating for today and tomorrow."

Namba explains that part of the district's mission includes getting devices in kids' hands, but by itself that wasn't good enough. If they really wanted to empower and motivate, they needed to do more. The community had expressed the need for connectivity, but also that people couldn't afford it. So the school district, in order to empower and motivate, created a free wifi network for the entire community. The kids now have what they need to succeed. Not only that but the district has also eliminated grade levels, instead focusing on what learning the student is ready for.

What is your personal mission statement for education in your area of expertise? Write it in the space below. If it doesn't fit on one line, is it worthwhile? If you have to "look it up", you're doing it wrong! After you've written it, share it on social media with a hashtag.

Your vision

You're not reading this book so you can lead just another school. You want to be a transformative leader. But how can you be transformative if you don't know what you are transforming into? Are scores the most important thing to you? Relationships? Attendance? When you have a vision, the people will follow.

A vision also requires you to say no to certain things. I learned this lesson when I was at my third school as an administrator. I mean, I knew this instinctually, but I let "shiny-object syndrome" and my own weaknesses get in my way. I'm going to walk you through what I did, not because I'm a genius, but because I applied what I learned from everyone I have interviewed in the three Transformative Leadership Summits I have organized and in my *Transformative Principal* podcast.

First, I took my time. This is the hardest part! If you're anything like me, patience is an elusive beast. I want everything to happen right now. After I got the job at the school, I pondered, asked questions, and learned as much as I could before I had to actually step into the role. The vision for my school became "What is needed, when it's needed." This simple statement encapsulates everything we do.

Second, I communicated my vision in simple terms. I communicated it to my boss, to make sure it aligned with her vision, and then I communicated it with my staff, when the time came for that.

Third, I communicated the vision again and again, until it was clear to others what actually needed to happen.

Fourth, I didn't care about the path people took to get there, just the end goal. This is also challenging. Vision is a destination, not a process.

The educational consultant and author Bob Sonju has talked to me about having a vision that compels people to action. If your vision is lackluster or doesn't inspire people, it will be very difficult to get people to take action to achieve that vision. They will continue doing things the way they have always done them. Sonju also talks about consensus and commitment. These are two different things. As a DuFour-trained educator, Sonju says that consensus means we all know what the plan is, while commitment means we are determined to get there. And when there is consensus, we are able to move forward even without 100% commitment. People who aren't committed to the vision will either get onboard and become committed, or self-select themselves out of the school. Perhaps most importantly, Sonju says, we must remember that "teachers work hard and enter the school every day with the best intentions of helping kids." Just because a teacher isn't committed doesn't mean they can't participate in the consensus of the vision and still provide value.

At my school we certainly had detractors (there will always be detractors), but we still pursued the vision. After I laid out my vision, I described to my staff the steps it would take to get there. I broke down the vision of giving kids what they need when they need it into smaller steps that could be handled more easily.

At the time, our district was doing a big push on personalized learning. We had hired a consultant and my vision aligned with personalizing learning for our students, but we were a very traditional school, doing things in the old way. In order to achieve the vision, we needed to adjust some structures. So our four-year plan was developed:

- **Year 1**: personalized learning aspect in one lesson/unit each quarter; prepare for flexible learning block.
- **Year 2**: personalized learning aspect every month (semester 1); implement flexible learning block; personalized learning aspect every other week (semester 2); pilot personalized learning plan for each student.
- **Year 3**: personalized learning aspect in each lesson; expansion of flexible learning block; personalized learning plan for each student.
- **Year 4**: no bell schedule; student-driven, standards-based lessons based on data, student need, and preference.

A couple of things to note. The vision of one personalized learning aspect in each quarter was the only requirement for the first year, apart from preparing for a flexible learning block, but that was pretty minimal. The amazing thing is that when people knew where we were headed, they jumped in with both feet. Many of them did much more than one personalized learning aspect and were very successful with what they put in place. They were able to go at their own pace.

Clearly, we didn't meet our Year 4 vision in the first year. I worked with the administrator Damon Hargraves on this and he described the vision as a mountaintop that we were both trying to get to. When we knew the mountaintop was our destination (and we also knew how incredibly far away it was), we could focus our own energies on getting there. Damon might decide to take a boat as far upriver as possible and then proceed on foot. I might take the hiking path. What's more important is that we check in with each other periodically to make sure we are still on track and our focus is in the right place. If Damon stops to build a log cabin on the way, he's lost direction. We are building the house on the mountaintop, not in the valley!

The yearly goals in the four-year plan make sure that we are all checking in, so we know that we are going in the right direction, on our own path. Here's the reality of what happened in my school. Some of my staff started out for a long, leisurely walk. Some of my staff got a car and started driving to the mountaintop. Some of my staff rode a horse. Others needed to be carried in a covered wagon – the equivalent of doing the bare minimum. But those teachers did, in fact, do one personalized learning activity each quarter, which was the expectation, and they did it as best they could. There weren't (and didn't need to be) any hard feelings about them not going fast enough.

The thing that is most amazing to me is that when we ran into problems, or people started planning something, they would actually ask, "Does this meet our vision of where we want to go?" If something didn't meet the vision, they kicked it to the curb! When the vision was clear, the staff made the right choices. For example, we had some chairs right inside the front door of the school where kids could sit. They broke and we needed to buy new ones. The head secretary was talking to a custodian about what kind of chairs we should get. The custodian suggested some really uncomfortable ones and the head secretary countered with some very comfy chairs. The custodian said something to the effect of, "Well, we don't want them just hanging out because it's comfortable." To which the secretary replied, "If what they need is a comfy space, then we should let them have one." Without intervention from me, she knew that we wanted to give kids what they need, when they need it.

When the coronavirus closures happened at the end of Year 3, the school was prepared for virtual learning and a different approach. They adapted quickly and with minimal challenges. When the school had a vision for where they were going, they were able to react to the global pandemic in a positive, student-focused way.

Creating your vision

If you don't have a vision for your school, all hope is not lost. Here are four things you can do to start developing your vision.

1. **Answer one question.** The education consultant Tom Hierck asks: what's the one thing you want someone to know about your school?

It can't just be about a specific leader's desire; it has to be rooted in the district vision, if applicable, and it has to align with what teachers are willing to buy into and what families want. Hierck also encourages us to ask: what makes us unique or special? This can help to identify the starting point. Imagine if someone was hired to be the president of the University of Kentucky or the University of North Carolina, and they thought basketball was a waste of a university's time. Do you think that person would fare very well or very long in that position? I sure don't!

2. **Ask your teachers what they think.** As I do my listening from spring break to August, I follow the advice of the elementary school principal Chris Wejr. He says that he regularly meets with teachers one-on-one. He also suggests one of my favorite activities, which is the SSC interview. In meetings with each member of your staff, ask them the following questions: what should we start doing? What should we stop doing? And what should we continue doing? As you ask these questions, you will hear the same ideas about what needs to be done at your school. Here's a quick leadership hack: if your team bring up the same things again and again, your school probably already has a vision. That's great. Buy into the vision that is already there and figure out how to take the team to the next level. In my school, the teachers repeatedly said, "We want to be known for doing something innovative."

3. **Simplify.** Vision statements and mission statements are too often overblown and written through committee. There are usually too many five-dollar words that can overcomplicate and obscure your vision. Use simpler words. Our vision is intentionally brief and vague: we give kids what they need, when they need it. It can be anything. If you are giving a student something they need, when they need it, it is easy to know you are doing the right thing. A simple statement can be very powerful.

4. **Test it out.** Start communicating the vision in everyday language. If it compels people to action, you're doing it right. If it doesn't, keep adjusting it until people start taking action. That's how you know it works.

Hierck told me, "I have yet to meet an adult or a student who is connected who doesn't want to give their all to the mission." Sometimes people aren't connected and don't want to buy into the vision you are offering. You can't get hung up on that. But if *nobody* is buying into it, you may be off-base. That's why you test it and see what you get from it. Hierck also adds that we should expect some people to not be there, yet. It's OK for someone to not be totally bought into your vision. Again, we are looking for consensus, which means everyone knows where we are going.

Your purpose

As a leader, you can run around like a chicken with your head cut off, or you can be proactive in the way that you approach your work. The key here is recognizing what your purpose is. Are you all about student learning? That's the easy one! Are you all about supporting your teachers? Are you all about sports and activities?

Finding your purpose sounds like a spiritual walk that many of us may not be accustomed to. Furthermore, we look at the leader experience and we think the easy answer is high levels of student learning. And while that is important, there are limits to your ability to impact student learning directly, as you are not a teacher. So, is your purpose as a leader *really* to improve student learning? What does that look like for you?

Is it possible that your purpose is to get out of teachers' way and empower them?

Is it possible that your purpose is to coach teachers so they can improve student learning?

Is it possible that your purpose is to be a judge, to keep "naughty" kids out of teachers' classrooms so they can focus on teaching kids who actually want to learn?

In order for us to move our schools forward, we must have a purpose for what we are doing. Bob Sonju also says we must create systems that are so powerful that people will be forced to learn what they need to learn.

Let's try a thought experiment. Let's say you are a principal in a school that is doing OK, but there are many kids who are not getting the education they should. Students from low-income homes rarely perform at grade level, and students from non-dominant backgrounds and those with disabilities are rarely, if ever, able to access the material they need to be successful. You get a new superintendent and in the first meeting the superintendent says, "I don't want to rock the boat. I just want everyone to know they are doing a great job, and we will be doing the same work we are doing today in five years." How inspired are you to change what you're doing to meet the needs of your struggling students? Not very, I imagine!

Now consider another scenario. Dave Doty, my superintendent when I took a district-level job, was so inspiring that I was willing to do just about anything to be in the same district as him. He set a five-year goal that was so challenging, yet attainable, that I wanted to be around him and see what he was going to do. It was not just that we were going to do some neat things – we were really going to change education. The power in his approach was that it compelled us to action.

The consultant and author Anthony Muhammad told me that people change when the dissatisfaction with the status quo is high enough. People have to get mad to be willing to change. You don't want to make people upset with you, but you want to give them a vision that is so great that they will want to be on your team as you accomplish the vision together.

Managing your time

Once you have a vision in place, you need to spend your time wisely to accomplish it. I'm going to share a story that is likely something you have encountered or will encounter as a principal.

Lindsey Martin (not her real name) wanted to be a teacher because she loved literature. She could talk about it all day, and she usually did. Her English class consisted entirely of what she wanted to talk about. Obviously, this created some frustration in kids who couldn't understand what made Emily Brontë so incredibly amazing in the 1800s. One day, a student pushed Mrs. Martin too far by stealing a pencil. Apparently it had happened a couple of times before, but she hadn't overreacted – she had tried to keep calm and continue discussing the merits of Victorian literature. But on this day, enough was enough. She marched all the students down to the office, where they would sit until the guilty party 'fessed up to the assistant principal.

As 35 squirrelly eighth-graders sat in the office, waiting for their teacher to finish explaining the gravity of the situation to the AP, he squirmed, and so did they. He had been pulled off a serious drug investigation to deal with this "crisis." Mrs. Martin had already made it clear to the class and secretary that she was not leaving until someone gave up the pencil.

How would *you* handle this situation?

To his credit, the AP kept his cool, lectured the students briefly about the importance of honesty and integrity, and sent Mrs. Martin and the kids back to class with a promise that if a student came forward in private, the repercussions would be lessened. Honestly, he didn't want to discipline anyone.

In our work as educators, there are many different events, people, and duties all vying for our attention. It is not only difficult but very awkward to try to determine who or what gets the attention. A good rule of thumb is, if someone asks if you have time for a "quick question," they need five minutes at least. If someone asks if you "have a minute," they need at least 15!

How do we decide where to direct our energies? One theory of leadership involves the Eisenhower matrix, which I have found very helpful.

EISENHOWER MATRIX

	URGENT	LESS URGENT
IMPORTANT	DO	PLAN
LESS IMPORTANT	DELEGATE	ELIMINATE

Delegation

The task list for a principal is plain ridiculous. Because this job is focused on working with people, the list of what you "need" to do is so long that nobody can ever actually accomplish it. We all know that, yet we think that we can be the one to finally accomplish it.

One of the most challenging aspects of the Eisenhower matrix is deciding what you should delegate to someone else. Delegation can be very scary, because you are putting someone else's name on the work that you are responsible for. I get it!

That fear of delegation can be reduced when you recognize that you already delegate the most important job in the school: teaching. You are the instructional leader for your school, yet you delegate the instruction of students to someone else (to multiple people, even!) every single day. If we can delegate a job as important as that to other people, surely we can delegate some of our other responsibilities as well.

Most people delegate poorly because they don't focus on the three main drivers of good delegation: teach explicitly, observe early, follow up regularly. For delegation to work effectively, you must first know how it needs to be done (or if the "how" is flexible, what the desired outcome is). Once you know what you want it to look like, you must teach it explicitly. If it is not taught explicitly, people will do their best, but it won't be what you want. Second, you must observe the results early. Let the person do the process once before you give feedback and stay with them as they are learning it. Third, you must follow up regularly. They may be showing proficiency, so give them room to fly, but be sure to check in regularly, in a planned way, to make sure they are accomplishing what you need them to.

There are three kinds of tasks that can be delegated. First, repetitive, low-level tasks that require very little thought or can be taught simply and easily. This would include tasks like:

- Running any kind of report (budget, transportation, tardy, attendance, grade point average, etc).
- Calling students down to the office.
- Calling parents about absent students (many districts use a robocall to ensure parents get a consistent, clear message about their child's attendance).

These tasks are often delegated to secretaries and other non-certified personnel, sometimes even students. Here's a way to delegate fetching students to a student aide.

- **Teach explicitly**: walk with the student aide to the classroom of the other student. Explain the importance of respecting the educational process and the teacher's classroom. Explain how you want the student to enter the classroom and how you want them to get the student's or teacher's attention. Explain how you want them to respond after the fact. Role-play the scenario with the aide and then model the action in the classroom. Ensure the expectations are written down and given to the student aide so she can review them later.
- **Observe early**: after you show the aide how to do it, allow her to do it herself while you watch, so you can give feedback on whether or not it was done correctly.
- **Follow up regularly**: every once in a while, check in with the aide to observe and make sure she is doing things correctly, and give feedback on how to improve further.

The second type of task that can be delegated is infrequent, important jobs that must be done in a certain way. This includes activities like the following:

- Transportation.
- Cross-walk duty.
- Various reports that the district office asks for.
- Teacher evaluations.

The third is regular, high-level, important tasks where the way they are done is not as important as the fact that they *are* done. The most obvious is teaching. Teaching is high-level, very important, and many different styles of teaching can be effective in reaching students. You don't have to be exactly like your next-door teacher to be just as effective. Other tasks like this include:

- Discipline.
- Counseling.
- Coaching teachers in instruction.

We talked about vision and purpose first because if you want to know what you need to delegate, you need to be clear on your purpose first and foremost. I created a vision for my school that included where we were heading in four years' time and focused on our personalized learning journey. In order to meet my vision for what our school could become, I needed to focus all my efforts on improving our teachers' skill in personalized learning and leave just about everything else behind. So, I know first-hand that it's challenging to have to delegate things you aren't really comfortable delegating.

Papers, papers, papers

When a principal is at a school for a long time, he collects certain things. As he prepares to move on, he thinks that the next principal will surely need all the files, notes, training materials, and little scraps of knowledge that he can't take with him to his new school. When I was doing my internship, I watched a retiring principal head out and his replacement come in. He had been at the school for a long time and had done his best to keep things organized, and he understood where things were and what was important. The problem was that there were many things that *weren't* really important that were inherited by his successor. There were so many extra papers that her filing space doubled when she finally gave up and threw his things away.

In most principals' offices, it would be easy to find little folders of papers that the principal thought would be important, but ended up not being important at all. We often save papers because we think we might need them. When I was growing up, the mom of a good friend would always say, "A place for everything, and everything in its place!" I know she didn't come up with that, but her immaculate home embodied that saying.

If you have a clear vision, and are spending your time on things that support your vision, you will be more successful in passing the important things on to the next principal.

Batching

I learned an important principle from the entrepreneur and author Michael Hyatt. I'm a big fan of Hyatt and I use many of his tools to help me work more effectively. One of those tools is batching: the grouping of similar tasks in order to streamline their completion. But batching can be challenging when you are the principal of a school, because everything seems like an emergency.

Multitasking is a myth. The leadership coach Peter Bregman, in an article for *Harvard Business Review*,[3] states that when we attempt to focus on multiple things at once, our productivity diminishes by as much as 40%. We may think we are able to multitask, but we just can't. We are simply switching from one task to another, very rapidly and ineffectually! Focusing on one thing until that is accomplished produces great gains.

A specific batching strategy that you may have heard of is the pomodoro technique. This is where you set a timer and complete a task or series of tasks in that specific timeframe. It's a pretty simple technique and doesn't take long to master. The key is to get your tasks done without getting distracted.

Start by writing down what needs to be done. This step is important, because tracking what you're doing makes a difference. Then set a timer for 25 minutes (or however long suits you) and work through your list. Your goal is to complete as much as you can, but you may not get through it all. When you complete the 25-minute stint, check off the things you have completed, note the number of times you were distracted, and take a five-minute break. Finally, after you've completed four pomodoro sessions, take a longer, 20-minute break.

Your attention span and ability to focus may be different than others, so pay attention to that. For me, pomodoro sessions are most effective at about 45 minutes. I just start itching for a change after 45 minutes, so I get up and walk around, and then I can get back in business. It could be a coincidence that I was on 45-minute periods in my first teaching position.

There are three good reasons to use batching.

---

3   Peter Bregman, "How (and Why) to Stop Multitasking," *Harvard Business Review*, 2010, tinyurl.com/rcz3s42

1. **Batching helps you to stay focused on what matters**. When you batch your like tasks together, you are able to focus just on those tasks for the time being. You know that you have time set aside for other things and you can deal with those then. You are able to focus on what is in front of you right now, and not be distracted by the million other things that are vying for your attention.
2. **Batching allows you more white space for creativity**. Batching means you can focus on what is needed at the time, so that when the moment comes for creativity, you know those nagging tasks will be accomplished in their appropriate slot. When you don't have to think about the other things on your task list, you can take the time you need to be creative in solving other problems.
3. **Batching helps you to be available for others**. One of my biggest pet peeves is talking to someone while they are banging out an email or doing something else on their computer. That is a clear signal to me that what I am saying is not as important as whatever they are doing.

I'd like to share some specific areas where I batch tasks to be more effective and make time for other things.

First, I batch for coaching and working with teachers. This time is in the mornings. Our schedule is set up so that all teachers have prep in the morning at least once a week, so I can spend that time working with them one-on-one or in groups. I feel that this is my most important work – my one thing I should do if nothing else ever gets done.

Second, I batch for district work. Tuesday afternoons are always set aside for doing the usually mundane things the district needs me to do.

Third, I batch for K12 magnet research. I am currently in the research phase of opening a first-of-its-kind K12 magnet school, so I batch that on Thursday mornings. My team knows that I will be unavailable for anything else at this time.

Here's the beauty of batching at set times: if I get something "urgent" from the district, I can tell them that I can have it to them by the end of Tuesday. This gives people an idea of when I can get the task done and I have no need to apologize for not getting it done sooner. And when I have an idea for the K12 magnet, I can make a note to pay attention to it on Thursday morning and then put it out of my mind.

Things that are challenging to batch

There are some parts of your job that are really difficult to batch. For example, checking email is probably a daily occurrence, though I would argue heavily that it is not an all-day occurrence. If you need to be in your email all day, that is a problem! Don't make that mistake. You should check your email every day, but you should set aside time for it.

Don't check email first thing in the morning. Wait. Check it after a couple of hours to ensure that your important work gets done. Since I am usually in teachers' classrooms in the mornings, my teachers and staff know they can grab me during that time to chat about anything they need. My emails usually take me about 30 minutes to process, and it is quite easy to make it work when I am out and about all the time. When I am not out and about, I feel like I get stuck doing the email thing all the time, and I never seem to get out of it. You can do some batching of email by setting aside that 30 minutes a day.

Another thing that is difficult to batch is student discipline. When a student makes a bad choice, it is easy to drop everything and go take care of that. But most of the time you can leave those student issues to cool for a few minutes, and often that is the better option. Of course there are exceptions, where your best-laid plans don't go how you want them to. The simple solution is to make sure that you calm yourself before reacting. Because I am in classrooms in the morning, those behavior issues typically need to wait until the afternoon. When I talk with kids later in the day, they have less time to waste. They are usually pretty quick to get to the root of the issue because they would rather be doing something else!

Parent communications and newsletters are sometimes difficult to batch, because you want your newsletters to be timely and full of fresh information. One way to make this process easier is to use a template. My template for parent newsletters is simple and I send it out weekly. There is an announcement of some action I want parents to take, a spotlight on personalized learning, a video from our news team, and one other interesting thing. It could be a link to an article or some other food for thought. It could be just something nice to say! Following this template means parents receive a consistent message from me and helps me to complete the newsletter very quickly.

Connected to this are positive phone calls to parents. There are some things that you will want to do daily, or as frequently as possible. Setting up routines or processes will dramatically decrease the time you need to devote to these endeavors. For example, if you want to make positive phone calls each day, a great strategy is to record the phone number of the student you want to call, along with the message, in your task management system. This means the phone call is shorter and easier to make, because the hard work of finding a number and knowing what to say is already taken care of.

Megabatching

Megabatching is where you deal with a whole-lotta-something, rather than just one small part of it. I could megabatch my email, sending and replying to all my emails on Thursday afternoons and not touching email again until the next Thursday. That probably wouldn't be acceptable in my district, but it is an example of megabatching. My district work and K12 magnet research are good examples of megabatching because I am trying to get a lot done during those times. Batching coaching is an example of something that I do daily, but I attempt to make it all happen at the same time, rather than having a coaching meeting, then an IEP, then a student conversation, then another coaching conversation.

Other things to consider as candidates for megabatching are tasks that are highly repetitive or formulaic. Reviewing parts of evaluations or scheduling evaluations are good examples of this. Rather than spreading observations over an entire month, crank down and get the observations done in a week – all of them. Imagine how much more fulfilled you would be if you did them all in a short amount of time like that!

Another good thing to megabatch is planning for professional development for the year. Rather than taking an hour each week to prepare staff meetings, plan out an entire month or quarter of staff meetings and have those plans clearly laid out. When the time comes,

Plan Your Week

	Sunday	Monday	Tuesday	Wednesday	Thursday	Friday	Saturday
05:00 - 05:30							
05:30 - 06:00							
06:00 - 06:30							
06:30 - 07:00							
07:00 - 07:30							
07:30 - 08:00							
08:00 - 08:30							
08:30 - 09:00							
09:00 - 09:30							
09:30 - 10:00							
10:00 - 10:30							
10:30 - 11:00							
11:00 - 11:30							
11:30 - 12:00							
12:00 - 12:30							
12:30 - 13:00							
13:00 - 13:30							
13:30 - 14:00							
14:00 - 14:30							
14:30 - 15:00							
15:00 - 15:30							
15:30 - 16:00							
16:00 - 16:30							
16:30 - 17:00							
17:00 - 17:30							
17:30 - 18:00							
18:00 - 18:30							
18:30 - 19:00							
19:00 - 19:30							
19:30 - 20:00							

the faculty meetings are more focused and connected, rather than one-and-done spray-and-pray!

One more candidate for megabatching is probably counterintuitive: once a month, I spend a day chatting and asking questions of my staff. I spend about 15 minutes with each person, scheduled, in my office, and it takes the whole day. But this helps teachers and staff to know that they will have my full attention, even briefly, on a regular basis.

The intangibles

While I was in the process of preparing the Transformative Leadership Summit: School Experience, I was also preparing to take a new job as a principal in Fairbanks, Alaska. It can be very beneficial to have a fresh start at a new school. Although I was a good principal at my previous school in Kodiak, I made a lot of mistakes and it was very challenging. And although I am still a good principal, I still make a lot of mistakes and get in my own way at times.

At my new school, the vast majority of my changes involved what I call "the intangibles." These are the areas where you can't really measure what you're doing. You can get to Inbox Zero and measure that, but you don't often measure your *tone* on the emails that you send to get to Inbox Zero. Another intangible area is culture. The culture in a building is a delicate ecosystem that takes lots of care and support.

And what about vision? A favorite proverb of mine is "Where there is no vision, the people perish." It doesn't matter how great your culture is if you don't have a vision for where you want to go. The culture doesn't help you to get there.

And then there's support – both the support you get as a leader and the support you give. Support doesn't mean saying, "Yes, you're right." Support often means saying, "That's not aligned with our vision."

Dissent is yet another intangible that we need to pay attention to.

Schoolmanship is another.

Empathy.

Communicating the why.

Relationships.

Acknowledging weaknesses.

Trust.

Strengths-based leadership.

Honestly, even as I write this, I get overwhelmed. This is too much to think about! Well, actually, it's not. Next, I'll be guiding you through these intangibles, and I'll be talking to some great leaders to see what we can learn from them on these subjects.

What I really want you to get from this is the idea that you don't need to be perfect. What you need to do is be your best, as often as you can. There are so many different ways to be successful, and you don't have to be like me or any other principal to be your best. It's about you creating an environment where your teachers, your students, and you can flourish. I really believe that you can do it.

Let me start with a brief story. Between the Transformative Leadership Summits I have organized and the *Transformative Principal* podcast I've been hosting since 2013, I have interviewed well over 300 effective, inspiring leaders. At the end of each interview, I ask guests on my podcast the same question: "What is the one thing a principal can do this week to be a transformative principal like you?" The responses have been so varied and every time I finish the interview I think, "Wow, I want to be just like that principal! That was amazing!"

Well, guess what? I'm not going to be and I never will be just like that principal.

Instead, I've taken a little inspiration from each person I have interviewed and tried to do better in that one area. Sometimes this has led to monumental change for me. Other times, I've tried and realized it isn't for me.

In 2015 I interviewed Rob Carroll, who was principal of South Heights Elementary in Henderson, Kentucky, at the time. Rob shared with me that he made home visits to all students before school started. I knew that was something my staff and I could do at our school in Kodiak, and I knew it would be beneficial. So, we did it. The scheme was voluntary for teachers and we ran it the day before new-teacher orientation. All the new teachers came and some veteran teachers, too. But not everyone. We did it in our own style and differently than Carroll did his home visits. Nevertheless, the purpose was the same: we wanted kids to know that we cared about them.

This was in my second year at that school, and we had better relationships and better behavior that year because the kids knew that we cared. It was really powerful. When the students had their teachers visit them at home before school started, they were excited to come to school. The home-visit scheme was also compounded by our study and awareness of adverse childhood experiences. We approached our students with a level of respect and support.

What's the point of this story? Well, it's pretty hard to measure all the things that made that year so successful, but it was truly amazing. There were a few things that catapulted teachers to success they had never seen before. Because we took a risk on visiting all 435 student homes, teachers knew they could take risks on connecting with kids. Because we cared about kids, kids cared about us. Because we had a vision for reaching out and letting kids and families know we cared, we had more positive relationships throughout the year. At least, it felt that way. Again, it's so hard to measure – and it often *isn't* measured.

As we discuss these intangibles, reflect on your skills, dispositions, abilities, strengths, and weaknesses. Don't try to be the people you learn about here; find a way to be *your* best.

Relationships

My sister shared a video with me from the TV talk show *Ellen*. The host, Ellen DeGeneres, spoke to a principal named Akbar Cook[4] about a super-cool idea to have washing machines in his school. But there was more to the story that Ellen only lightly touched on.

The relationships that Cook forms with his students are amazing. He is the principal of West Side High School in Newark, New Jersey. His school is located in what he calls the "number blocks," which is "where bad things usually happen." Students have to navigate gang-inhabited areas to get to school.

In the video, Cook says, "Some of my babies were homeless. Other babies are coming from homes where there's no parent, where they cannot wash clothes in their house." Note that he calls his students

---

4   "Ellen Meets Extraordinary New Jersey Principal Akbar Cook" (video), *The Ellen Show*, 2018, youtu.be/O1P6oZjfR54

"my babies." You can hear in his voice that they really are his babies. A student in the video says, "A person like Cook, you don't really wanna let him down." He has a relationship with those students that runs deep.

"I just try to give so much love," he says, "that they give it back to me." Cook comes from the same community as his students and says he isn't going anywhere.

Some people in education argue that we shouldn't tell our students we love them, or let them say they love us. Different people will have different perspectives on that argument. But I'll tell you, with all that is going on in our world, we could really use more love. We could really use more acceptance. We could really use more kindness and compassion.

Hamish Brewer is a principal in Virginia. In a video on YouTube,[5] he talks about how he wants to disrupt education and about his frustration with the norm. As he prepares to join a new school serving many low-income families, he says, "These kids have people revolving in and out of their lives. I have to be the constant … If this [school] doesn't change, I've failed a community, I've failed children … I can't fail them. That's not an option."

Brewer is always that intense. I've met him in person twice, and both times his tone and his intensity were the same, whether we were talking about school reform, skateboarding (his other passion), or anything else.

"Everything I do is about kids. Every decision I make comes back to: was I better for kids today?" he says in the video. He adds that, in his schools, "you're either in our gang or you're not. There's no opting out of what we want to achieve."

Cook and Brewer have many things in common, but the most important is that they love their students. Brewer starts the day by saying over a loudspeaker, "If someone didn't tell you today they love you, Mr. Brewer is telling you today he loves you."

I think most educators love their students, but some are hesitant to say so, or to act that way. Some principals think they need to be the disciplinarian first. That's just backwards. Whether you tell the kids you love them or not, everything you do in a school hinges on relationships.

---

5   "The Tattooed, Skater Principal Making Education Fun Again" (video), Freethink, 2017, youtu.be/VKt9CslbVsg

If you don't have good relationships, your school is not going to make much of an impact. That's just the plain truth.

Difficult conversations

The author and consultant Jennifer Abrams told me that a relationship is a prerequisite when it comes to making a success of hard conversations. Having a hard conversation with someone you don't have a relationship with is most likely going to fail. As it relates to students, she says, "A culture of yelling and bullying is not something we want to model for kids."

Jeff Zoul takes this to another level, asking principals to have pointed conversations with staff about what is happening in the school and to make sure everyone is doing what is right for kids. I love the three questions he suggests we ask: "What are we good at? What do we need to get better at? And how can you help?" He starts by valuing the opinions and expertise of his staff, and encourages them to provide input and help to tackle the challenges.

Zoul suggests that we "address underperformance by everybody." (And there is power in calling it underperformance, because it inspires people to live up to their potential.) But how can you maintain good relationships if you are addressing underperformance? By continuing to build the relationship, Zoul says, and using the correction as a way to say, "I care enough about you to make sure that you know that what you are doing is underperforming."

This is a challenge for me, too! It's not just you, or that other principal you know. I have three tips to help you get started on difficult conversations tomorrow.

1. **Apologize**. It's likely that you have made the hard conversation necessary because you didn't say something when you should have. So start by saying, "I'm sorry." Let your teacher know that you have not been fair to them by neglecting to address areas of underperformance earlier.
2. **Address the behavior, not the person**. This is something we do with kids all the time, but adults can react in the same way

as kids. They think we are making a personal judgment against them if we say something critical. So, focus your efforts on the behavior, not the person. One way that I deal with teachers being late to classes, staff meetings, or anything else is by saying, "Welcome, I'm glad you're here." Later, when I can talk with them in private, I reiterate that I am glad they came, but that it would be more appropriate if they were there on time. Often, they want to make an excuse for why they were late, but I never need an excuse. I say, "I trust that you would have been here if that thing hadn't happened. I just want you to know that I value your contributions as a member of the team, and I want you to be here and be professional by being on time." This usually goes over pretty well, and people know that I am serious about this expectation of being on time.

3. **Celebrate successes**. When people do something awesome, be sure to celebrate it with them. Zoul says this is an essential part of your toolkit in addressing underperformance and other weaknesses.

Praise

Zoul is surprised by how worried people are about praising. As leaders, we should be praising nearly every good thing we see. Not because you just want to say nice things, but because there is a lot of good stuff happening in your school! Don't fear it – be part of it.

Most principals are worried about praising people because teachers are notorious for cutting off the head that gets above the others. Why? I don't know, but it sure is sad. We are so much better when we are working together and supporting each other.

"Kids are so perceptive. They know if the adults collaborate or like each other," Zoul told me. He explained that we may think we are keeping our feelings about our colleagues well under wraps, but the reality is that kids see right through our facade.

Once, I was working with a group of teachers who were not collaborating, trying to iron out their personality conflicts. We were having conversations behind closed doors and they were being "professional" with each other, which was really a code word for "not professional". When some students and I were talking in the cafeteria about how classes were going, one student asked bluntly, "Why do Mrs. Smith and Mrs. Terry hate each other?" Shocked, I responded, "What do you mean?"

He said, "Well, they don't talk to each other like our other teachers, and any time Mrs. Terry comes by Mrs. Smith, Mrs. Smith walks away. You can tell they don't like each other. I just don't understand why."

That 11-year-old student's perception was astounding. There were hurt feelings, frustrations, and challenges, and to that student – and others – the problem was obvious.

Sometimes, Zoul says, we fear that praising staff might drive a bigger wedge between some teachers. Instead of avoiding giving praise because it might hurt someone else's feelings, we need to be constantly providing feedback – critical, constructive, and positive. If a day goes by when you don't praise your staff, you are missing an important opportunity.

Culture

Culture eats strategy for breakfast (according to the management guru Peter Drucker). You have to have the right culture in place to do anything meaningful in schools.

As we consider the culture of your school, the design-thinking process is very important. This is because, as the leader, you may not see clearly what it is that you are doing or not doing to impact on the culture.

How do you gain empathy about the ways that you are affecting your school's culture? I suggest empathetic interviewing. But you may need to enlist the help of others to do this, because some people may decline to tell you the truth, instead telling you what they think you want to hear.

Here are some questions that you can ask people. There are many more questions to ask, but these will be a good start in figuring out the culture in your school.

- What did you feel as you came into the school building?
- Did you feel welcome?
- Did you feel that this is a place for learning?
- What role do you feel students play in our school?

- What does the signage communicate to you as you enter the school?
- Were the front-office staff welcoming and inviting?

And some questions that you can ask yourself:

- When people approach our school, how is the curb appeal?
- Does the school exterior invite you to enter?
- What signs are displayed as you approach the school? Are they welcoming?
- As you enter the school, what do you see? Is it welcoming?
- Is student work displayed as you enter?
- What signage greets you as you enter?
- What people welcome you (or not)?
- Is it obvious where to go as you enter the school?

Anthony Muhammad wrote a book called *Transforming School Culture*[6] in which he describes how to overhaul your school culture. I'm not going to attempt to recreate or redo his amazing work, but I will touch on a couple of things here.

Culture is a huge project that is never fully completed. You need to approach it from many different viewpoints, but we will focus on the leader viewpoint in this section. As the school principal, everything that happens in your school, for good or evil, is a direct result of your leadership.

Let that sink in for a minute.

Yes, the work is long. Yes, the work is difficult. Yes, the work is challenging. But what can you do, as the leader, to make the school culture better?

First, know your people. In his book, Muhammad talks about the four different types of educator you can find in a school. I had the great pleasure of interviewing him for the Transformative Leadership Summit: School Experience and he spoke about the fundamentalist personality, whose organizational goal is to maintain the status quo. They are used to

---

6   Anthony Muhammad, *Transforming School Culture: how to overcome staff division*, Solution Tree, 2009

doing things in the way they have always done them and don't see a need to change their behavior. You can overcome their resistance to change by following four simple steps:

1. Explain the why (there's that vision piece again!).
2. Establish trust and create an emotional connection.
3. Teach the how, but avoid innovation fatigue.
4. Recognize that some people will always struggle with a new way of doing things.

Muhammad estimates that, when it comes down to it, there are really only one or two people on any given staff who can't actually do the work needed to change. But before you can get to step 4 and recognize who those people are, you need to do the other three steps. We talked about explaining your why earlier, so now let's look at establishing trust.

Building trust

One of the ways that I create trust is through relationships. In order to build relationships, Zoul says, we must have "real, active listening and pointed questions." Active listening is actually hearing what people are saying – and what they are *not* saying.

One of my favorite personal examples of this was a teacher who had been at the school for many years before I arrived. She was a vocal staff member, unafraid to express her opinion. She also knew that the school was ready for a change and wanted to ensure that could happen. When I asked her questions, or sought her opinion on something, she would answer very strategically, specifically and concisely. Because we had established trust, she knew that she didn't have to say everything on her mind, but could focus on the things that really mattered.

The elementary school principal Chris Wejr told me that it is vital to follow through on what we say we are going to do. It is easy to fall behind on an ever-increasing task list, but we must fight to overcome that. One way we can do that is by only adding things to our list that are truly important and necessary. Many things can be delegated and even passed back to the people asking for them in the first place. We've got to be focused on the things that we *can* do, not just the things everyone else wants us to do.

Dissent

Zoul has another suggestion for building trust: valuing diversity and dissent. He says that diversity of thought and dissent are not bad things. This is a delicate balance. He is quick to point out that staff members who dominate faculty meetings with constant pessimism are not offering the kind of dissent that builds trust and leads to positive change. Rather, allowing that negative behavior to continue undermines the trust you have built in a very corrosive way. Zoul stresses that we need people who complement us. If we all believe the same thing and there is no dissent, there will be underperformance by many, or people doing things for the wrong reasons.

I had an employee once who disagreed with everything I suggested. She was definitely my favorite employee. Any time I needed to see if something was a good idea, I would run it by her and she would give me the pulse on what other staff members would think but not say. She taught me how to break through defenses and give credibility to my ideas, because she helped to make them into plans, not just ideas. Later, when she and I parted ways, I wondered if I would ever have an employee who set me up for success so well.

You need to find and value that diversity and dissent. When you do, make sure the relationship with the dissenter is strong. But beware: some people will disagree just to try to bring you down. Be careful of those who go behind your back to question you and your ideas. People who do that are not likely to be on your side.

One way that I value dissent in my staff is that we have a norm of saying, "Yes, and… ." Much like in improv settings, you can kill an idea in no time by saying no. Instead, we respond "Yes, and…" and then give our thoughts.

Here's a good example. In a staff meeting, we are talking about a school-wide behavior plan and how to address certain things. One person argues that students should not have cell phones because they are on Snapchat and cyberbullying all the time. Another teacher responds, "Yes, the problem with social media use in school is real. We need to find a way to teach students how to use cell phones, because we all need these kids to do the work in our classes and we are a district-designated bring-your-own-device school." This person expressed her dissenting thought, but in a way that added to the conversation, rather than sparking an argument.

One-on-one connections

Zoul and Wejr both emphasize the importance of small, one-on-one conversations with staff about a variety of topics. These intimate conversations tell you what you really need to know about how people feel in your school. The more of this you do, the better. It can be easy to be overwhelmed with meetings and to-do lists, but making time for people and one-on-one conversations allows the bigger things to happen.

When I built the vision in my school, a big part of this was my intention to spend the first half of each day coaching teachers. I would observe their class, talk with them, be available, and answer questions. That made it much easier for them to do the things I needed them to do. Wejr suggests we develop commitments in staff meetings, but have individual conversations to measure, track, and improve those commitments.

Zoul also suggests that we build trust by being honest, calm, and respectful. As an administrator, it seems as if you are constantly putting out fires – and that can be a little stressful. It can cause even the best of us to get frustrated and overreact. I have intentionally developed some habits of de-escalation, where I do the opposite of someone who is getting upset. As they escalate, I speak more slowly, more quietly, and show less emotion, even if I am seething inside. It keeps me from yelling back at people, which is never productive.

And Zoul suggests that we never question the motives of teachers. Once I had a teacher who asked if I was making a change to our PLC processes because I thought people were wasting time. I replied that I continuously evaluated and checked our processes to make sure they were as successful as possible. I stressed that I didn't think staff wasted time, but that they could have better leadership in this area and be more successful. I took the responsibility for something not working and made sure she didn't think I was questioning the motives of teachers. Wejr adds to this thought by suggesting that we should be "hard on content, soft on people." Giving grace and assuming the best intentions of teachers and staff is a sure-fire way to make everyone more happy.

Bullying

There is one more area of culture that I want to address. It's a hard one to talk about and I was so grateful when Zoul addressed this topic in our conversation. This is the topic that we usually avoid at all costs, mostly because teachers, students, parents, and leaders are afraid of what happens when it is addressed.

Schools with teacher bullies are schools that have student bullies. I touched on this in the introduction.

Sometimes, those bullies are principals. If you are a principal and you are the bully, just stop it. There are educators out there who use their positional authority to bully and demean others. They do it to teachers, to admin, to students, to parents. The bullying is often passive-aggressive and sometimes hard to identify objectively. But that doesn't mean we should let it continue. It is not OK.

I heard from one person who was transferred to another position in the same district. She was elated that she didn't have to work with a "teacher bully" any more. I asked her why she had never told her principal about the struggles she went on to describe; she said that it would have been so much worse for her if she had. Isn't this the case with all bullies? They are empowered by the fear they set in the hearts of their victims. No matter what efforts we go to stop the bullying, we can't keep watch all the time. There will be moments when we don't see what they are doing, and they know it. So, the intimidation, coercion, and mean-spirited attacks continue until we can gather enough evidence to truly put a stop to it.

The challenge of confronting this issue does not mean we should ignore it. We should do our very best to make the right choices and support those we serve.

It's OK to make mistakes

Zoul suggests that when mistakes are made, we all get together, acknowledge the mistakes, and take ownership of them. This is a small step, but owning mistakes makes life so much easier. It takes the wind out of the sails of those who are blaming you anyway! That might be the best part of taking ownership. If you own the problem, people can point the finger all they want, but it doesn't have the same impact.

The educator Jon Harper has an excellent podcast called *My Bad*. In it, he interviews people who share a brief story about how they made a mistake, and what the ramifications of that mistake were. It's interesting to hear the mistakes that people share.

Sometimes, when I listen, I think, "That's not really a mistake!" Other times, I cringe and feel a great amount of empathy for the person in that situation. Here's the thing about owning your mistakes, big and small: Harper told me that admitting your mistakes actually shows strength. I couldn't agree more. When you admit your mistakes and take ownership, you show those around you that you have the confidence and courage to learn from a misstep.

New principals are especially susceptible to the lure of perfection. They think they need to maintain their authority. But not admitting your mistakes actually makes you look weaker and exposes your lack of self-confidence.

Harper has a few suggestions to make admitting mistakes a little easier. First, it's important to apologize. You've got to start there.

Second, acknowledge that you are going to make mistakes if you are living a passionate life. Taking fewer risks and making fewer decisions might mean you make fewer mistakes, but it won't help you to live a passionate and worthwhile life.

Third, be willing to offer grace to others. Don't approach someone about their mistake until you are sure that they are not doing anything to fix it. I had one teacher who made a lot of mistakes; he was always saying or doing something inappropriate around students. His mistakes were definitely a result of living a passionate life and trying to do cool things with the kids. Often, he overstepped, tripped up, or bit off more than he could chew. What was great, though, was that he would recognize the mistake, tell me about it, and show me what he was doing to make it better. It sure was hard to get mad at that guy, even though he caused me a lot of stress. I could handle it because I knew that he was working to make things better. He was putting in the effort.

According to Harper, there are three types of mistakes people usually make in education.

The first is not knowing the whole story. Nearly every time I try to take action on something, I think about this mistake. It is so easy to think that we have all the information, when we often don't. Whenever you're dealing with people, it is important to gain the perspectives of everyone involved. This extra step will save you grief later, because there is always grief when you don't have all the information.

The second type of mistake relates to power and ego. When you think with the part of your brain that is focused on self-serving behavior, you usually wind up making a misstep. These mistakes can happen to anyone and they are embarrassing to apologize for. People usually don't understand your motives, so then you have to apologize for the behavior, and when people don't understand, you feel obligated to explain why it was a bad move. I have many examples of times when I pulled an ego move and had to apologize later, explaining that I had acted that way because of my own ego. Talk about embarrassing. And it's worse if you have to apologize to a student!

The third type of mistake is the opposite of the second. Instead of making a mistake because you think you're so good, you make a mistake because of self-doubt. The BYUtv comedy show *Studio C* has a sketch where a young man is attempting to study for an exam. His distractions are personified and Self-Doubt tells him: "I'll always be here to make sure you question yourself with every choice you make." Self-doubt is a universal feeling that we all experience in our own way. The feeling is natural and normal, but the actions we take because of self-doubt need to be curtailed. You have to know that you are important and capable.

I'd like to share a story from my blog about when I made a mistake using Twitter in 2008. I have left this Twitter post up for all these years to remind me of the missteps I can take if I don't think before I post. I could have deleted it or made my posts private, but I decided that I wanted this post to be an example. Since then I've made more than 20,000 positive Twitter posts, which illustrates that if we are living a passionate life, our mistakes will eventually be buried by all the good works we are doing.

Here's an extract from my blog post[7] about the mistake; I've made minor edits to make sure the thoughts behind the words can shine through.

"It all started two months ago when I caught three girls cheating on a test. I made a poor decision and ripped up their papers in front of the class. Those three girls have been inciting the rest of the class for a couple months to near rioting. This class has been very difficult to deal with despite many long talks with many students. It is very frustrating. These students know exactly how I feel. Well, they should know. On Friday we had another talk about how they should behave and what is expected of them. Yesterday, I posted this on Twitter:

'Fire drill today with my worst class. Lucky me.'[8]

Whenever my students need an assignment, I direct them to my website and tell them to print things off my calendar. I have found out that a lot of them get to my website via search engines. What do you suppose is one of the results when you search for Jethro Jones? It is not my Twitter page. Nor does it rise to the top when you search for my name and the word Twitter. But somehow, the above Twitter post was one of the top results, because one of my students asked me today, 'Mr. Jones, why do you think we are your worst class?' I asked why she thought that, and she quoted the above Twitter post nearly perfectly and told me that her mom found it when trying to find my website. My class was surprisingly good for the fire drill, even though I didn't expect them to be that good. So, one other girl asked why I hate them, and after being corrected, asked why I dislike them. I explained that they are my worst-behaved class. It doesn't mean that I hate them or dislike them, but it does mean that they drive me crazy and that they can be very annoying. I told them this. I have not kept it a secret from them before now, and I have not tried to hide it from them. As I

---

7 Jethro Jones, "Twitter Backfires!", *Have a Good Life* (blog), 2008, tinyurl.com/5uxjxq
8 twitter.com/jethrojones/statuses/799550076

said, we have had many long chats about this. This girl's mom was not upset, or so the student said. She thought it was pretty funny, actually. The students were good today after another long chat. They also were much better at keeping the others on task. ·

Now that you have the background, here are my thoughts. First, why were they so upset about this despite the nearly hundreds of times I have talked to them about it? They all knew about the Twitter post before they came into my class, because this girl probably told them all about it in first period. I think they were upset because it was public on the internet and people could find it. They knew they had the fire drill yesterday, and so they finally understood that I thought they were my worst class (despite the fact that I have been trying to tell them that for weeks). Second, it is hard for these seventh-graders to disassociate negative things. Just because they are my worst class does not mean that I hate or dislike them. They don't understand that (hopefully) adults can separate the two feelings. I told them that they annoy and frustrate me, but that as soon as they are doing what they should, those feelings go away. Third, how in the world did she find that? My website was above all the possible Twitter statuses even when I searched for 'Jethro Jones Twitter'. I guess she could have found her way to my blog, but I don't know. Crazy. Fourth, this has definitely reminded me that what I write is available and can be found. I need to remember that. I don't usually post anything controversial, but even things like this, that can be found by the mom of a student in that class, are fair game."

From this experience, I learned that I should be aware of what I am posting. I also saw that I should focus on the positive with my students. Constantly complaining about my students was assigning blame to the wrong people. The blame needed to be directed at me! Once I was able to own that, I didn't need to blame kids any more.

One other example of a mistake I have made was when I was talking with a group of staff about the educator Todd Whitaker's advice that we make our decisions based on our best teachers.[9] My counselor was uncomfortable with my choice of words when I said, "We are not going to do the things that our bad teachers want, just because they are loud!" She later asked me if there were any bad kids. I told her I didn't believe that there were. She said, "Then are there bad teachers?" Of course, my answer could only be no. How could I believe there were bad teachers when I didn't believe there were bad kids? I needed better descriptors.

Now, I criticize the behavior, not the person. There are still adults who frustrate me, who push back for the sake of pushing back, and who don't teach effectively, but I am much better at distinguishing between them now, and I don't associate them with being bad just because they have a different opinion.

Strengths-based leadership

One amazing thing about being a principal is that we have this great opportunity to utilize the strengths of those we work with. You may think that strengths-based leadership is too difficult, but it really isn't. Here's how it works: you give people opportunities to do things that are in their area of strength.

I listen to a podcast by Michael Hyatt and Megan Hyatt-Miller called *Lead to Win*. In a recent episode, they talked about strengths-based leadership in the context of decorating the office and turning over the planning of an event to two other people. Both of these activities turned out way better than they could have imagined, because people who had strengths in those areas were doing the work and making the decisions.

I'd like to share an example from my own school that illustrates this. We asked our librarian, Tana Martin, to head up the planning for the first three days of school for students. Her strength is not in coming up with fun activities (she asked someone who did have a strength in that area to do that work). Instead, her strength is in details and communication. She defined what everyone's role was, where they needed to be and then communicated that clearly. She did the job so much better than I would have done.

---

9 Peter DeWitt, "What Great Educators Do Differently: A Conversation with Todd Whitaker," *Education Week*, 2011, tinyurl.com/ycm5n55l

When I coach principals on leading in this manner, they have some fears. One of those fears is that if they hand authority over to someone else, that person will mess it up or won't be able to handle it. Our librarian had similar concerns. She was afraid that she couldn't handle doing all that work and would struggle to get everyone on the same page. She was worried that she wouldn't be able to plan fun activities. She was also afraid that I would derail her plans with my own ideas.

We worked through those issues one at a time. First, we made sure she knew that her job wasn't to plan everything, but to be the point person for the three days. She delegated one day completely to a trainer we brought in. She delegated different parts of other days to different people (even delegating something back to me). She spotted the strengths of the assistant principal and delegated the running of a school-wide pep rally.

Communication about the first three days of school ran through her, and she was able to answer all questions and be very successful. She wasn't perfect (who is?) but she did a wonderful job in helping people to have a great first few days of school.

Another situation when we used strengths-based leadership relates to my assistant principal. Carla Marquand came to our school from the East Coast and had a lot of learning to do about our culture. What she didn't have to learn was good instruction and professional development. She arrived ready to take our math department down a new path, using inquiry to teach. It was really quite remarkable to see her step in and take hold of that group and move them to where they needed to be.

Had I not put the person with the strength in front of the right people, our math would have continued how it had in the past, which would have been fine. But we aren't OK with fine. We want excellence. We want continuous improvement. We want people who are doing the best work they can, all the time. By allowing people to use their strengths, we can be at our best as a team.

The other big question I get when coaching principals on strengths-based leadership is: how do I know what their strengths are?

This is also easier than you think. You pay attention to what people get excited about. Pay attention to what they work hard at. Pay attention to what gets done. Then ask them to do something and see how they perform.

Sometimes, you take a shot in the dark and find out that someone is *not* good at certain things. I had an employee once whose strength was in motivating people to get the work done, not in getting the work done. It was really cool to see how he could get people excited about a vision, and then give them support to do the work to get the job done. I saw success around him and put him in charge of completing some tasks. Not a good idea. That's how I learned that his strength was inspiring others.

Have you ever sat staring at a blank page, hoping that the words will suddenly come to you? That was this man's problem. He couldn't get started on something. So, to help, we made checklists and set boundaries to help him contribute and still take on a leadership role.

Another way to identify people's strengths is to use something like StrengthsFinder. The StrengthsFinder assessment tool tells you your top five strengths (out of 37) and using this in cooperation with something like DISC gives you even more information. I want to stress that these aren't the only tools you can use, but they give you a framework that helps you to have "three-point conversations" with your staff. Three-point conversations involve you, another person (or multiple people), and a document, set of data, or a framework. When you have these three-point conversations, it is a lot easier to not take things personally.

When people are working in their strengths, they are more happy and fulfilled. After having meaningful conversations with students, teachers, and parents all day, I often go home thinking, "Am I really getting paid to do this job?" I just love it that much. It doesn't seem like work to me.

Recognizing weaknesses

Hand in hand with strengths-based leadership goes recognizing weaknesses. It is important here to clarify that weaknesses don't mean you are a bad person. It so often feels like any weakness is a defining characteristic of who we are, more so than our strengths. We have to get over that line of thinking.

After teaching and before I became a principal, I worked in the district office, as a library supervisor and as a curriculum specialist. I'll admit, neither of those jobs suited me very well. I worked hard and did good things, because I have my own standards that I need to live up to, but those roles were not in my area of strength. For me to be successful, I need to be engaged in many conversations with many different people about many different topics. I need a fast-paced environment where there is a lot of flexibility and change.

There's a good way to determine what your areas of weakness are: ask yourself the following questions.

1. What things do you put off doing?
2. What areas of your work do you scramble to do at the last minute?
3. What do you just not like doing?
4. In what areas has feedback indicated a need for improvement?
5. When it comes to completing your work, what areas do you see that need the most improvement?

Rather than making a plan to improve your weaknesses (because we all have many), I strongly suggest that you make a plan to delegate your weak areas to someone else. Part of what made my job as a library supervisor so challenging was that the librarians didn't need the oversight that my position traditionally provided. They were seasoned veterans who knew how to do the work; the bureaucracy that our district was pushing on them was unnecessary. After a year, I worked myself out of the job by empowering the librarians to take more control over their own jobs. Part of my role was to approve building-level purchases at a district level before they were routed to the principal. It was an unnecessary step. So, we eliminated it.

Embrace your weaknesses

In our world, it is easy to think that everyone must be perfect or live up to some unattainable standard of excellence. What's very challenging is admitting that we are weak in areas. Don't be embarrassed by your weaknesses. Instead, seek a mentor who will support you and help you to find ways to overcome your weaknesses.

Being embarrassed is a choice, and a choice we make to our own detriment. It's a lot more embarrassing to have your weaknesses pointed out in an evaluation meeting when you've known all along that you struggle in that area.

Using your district's administrator evaluation tool, or principal leadership standards from national principal associations or anywhere else, assess yourself honestly and thoughtfully about where you may struggle. Find an area where you are comfortable seeking support to improve and ask someone you can rely on for help in doing that.

Sometimes, you just have to improve your weaknesses. In a secondary school environment where you have a lot more staff, it is pretty easy to find (and hire) people who have different skill sets to you, so you can delegate your weaknesses to others. In small schools, and sometimes by nature of your job, you just can't delegate things to others. I'd argue that you can delegate more often than you think, but sometimes there are things you just have to do.

The first way to start to improve your weaknesses is to share them. As you share them, you normalize them and they become less scary. Share them with your supervisor and make your own plan of how you will improve upon them.

Two areas where I really struggle are time management and detail-oriented work. Can you imagine how difficult this book has been to write? If you're reading it, you will know that I am overcoming a very big weakness in myself by publishing it!

You see, I used to write for a blog when I was a teacher and I got paid for it. It was pretty cool. I wrote about technology and I love technology. Well, you know what? That's the only job I've ever been fired from. How do you get fired from writing blog posts?

Well, I didn't pay attention to the details, and my thought processes were too grandiose for people to easily make connections in my writing. In my role as a principal, these weaknesses can be very challenging.

To overcome my weaknesses, I put processes and systems in place to help me know everything that needs to be done. I didn't put my librarian in charge of the planning for the first three days of school only because it was her strength, but also because it was my weakness. I knew that if I were in charge, it would take twice as long and cause 10 times as much frustration. I used my strengths (big-picture thinking, connecting people, communicating the vision, delegating) and took my weaknesses (scheduling, detail, organization) right out of my hands. I couldn't mess it up if I just left it alone.

What are some processes you can put in place to compensate for your weaknesses? Here's a thought exercise for you. In the space below, write down three weaknesses that prevent you from doing your most effective work (I'm doing the first one for you to model it).

1. Attention to detail.
2.
3.
4.

Below, write the skills needed to tackle that weakness effectively.

1. Create a task list of everything that could possibly need to be done (this is so hard for me).
2.
3.
4.

Let's remember that this is your area of weakness and your idea of what needs to happen is probably not going to come to you very easily. So, next to the corresponding number below, write the name of a person who could help you figure out how to overcome your weakness – or you could delegate to. If you can't think of a name, you would benefit from hiring someone with that skill set.

1. Tana, Courtney, David
2.
3.
4.

Now that you have identified your weaknesses, a strategy, and a person to help you, you are ready to talk with that person and tell them what you need from them. This can be awkward, but it is so worth it. Once you are no longer embarrassed by your weaknesses and you share them freely, something amazing will start to happen. Teachers, students, and support staff will start to acknowledge their weaknesses, too.

The power of mentors

Finding a mentor is not just important. It's vital if you want to be more than just another school principal. Michael Jordan didn't become a great basketball player by sheer force of will (although that helped), but rather because he was coachable and sought feedback. The same is true for principals. Great principals seek opportunities for coaching and growth.

That's precisely why I created a mastermind program for principals (jethrojones.com/mastermind). We meet once a week, for an hour on a video call, to ask each other questions, share our experience, and give honest feedback. It's the best professional development you'll ever experience, because it is timely, focused on making you better, and helps to identify your blind spots so you can be a transformative principal.

Here are the three major qualities I look for in a mentor.

1. **They ask questions**. Nobody likes being told what to do, but we do love figuring out our own solutions to our problems. You want someone who will ask you difficult and thought-provoking questions to help you find your next steps. I recently worked with a leader who was putting out figurative school fires left and right. As we asked questions and clarified what he was actually finding important, he quickly realized that the issues were the result of a bigger problem: he didn't paint a clear vision for his staff. At the next staff meeting, he articulated his vision and almost immediately the fires went out. His team no longer needed to ask questions about small things, because they could see the bigger picture and the direction they were headed in.

2. **They have the experience you need**. You want to find a mentor who has done things you want to do, or at least helped others to do so. This one can be tricky because you have to think in smaller steps. If you want to become the next Charlotte Danielson, Todd Whitaker or

Robert Marzano (or any other edu-celebrity), you don't necessarily need to get one of them to coach you, although it would be nice. You need someone who has done something similar, or helped someone else to do something similar. For example, Michael Jordan's coaches weren't the best basketball players before him, but they had experience in helping other players to succeed. Additionally, you can find someone well-connected to others who have achieved what you are trying to accomplish. As I mentioned earlier, I am currently at work on opening a first-of-its-kind K12 magnet school. Although we are only in the research phase, having connections to different innovative principals has been very helpful – they have provided me with valuable advice and resources as we plan this school.

3. **They provide honest feedback.** Early in my career, I was really struggling and I asked my mentor how others perceived me. He, thankfully, was very honest and helped me to figure out what was lacking in my professionalism. Later in my career, I interviewed for a position and asked for feedback from the superintendent. Again, he was brutally honest. It can be hard to hear negative feedback, but it is worth the discomfort. Both these mentors helped me to figure out what I was lacking and grow into a more effective leader. A person who cares more about your success than your ego can allow you to identify your weaknesses and become your best self.

Gaining empathy

On a recent school tour, I observed a principal teaching a class about empathy to his students. He showed a video about empathy interviewing. The kids were then able to conduct empathy interviews themselves to create something of value for another person. This was an interesting approach.

Principals can gain empathy in a number of ways, more than I could list here, but I would like to offer some ideas to get your own creative juices flowing.

1. **Shadow a student**. This simple practice can have lifelong implications for you as a school leader. The first time I followed

a student around my building, I was bored stiff. That was rough. Following the student around all day was a wake-up call about what instruction in my school looked like.

2. **Empathy interview**. An empathy interview is part of the design-thinking process. It's really quite simple: you ask questions to see what people want. By conducting the interview, you can learn so much about what people perceive about your school.

3. **Simple survey**. You can ask parents and students about what they are struggling with through a survey system, so you are asking everyone the same questions. I send a survey to my parents asking them how satisfied they are with our school. Then I ask them for open-ended comments. I have had some pretty remarkable responses that I would never have received had I not given them a voice.

4. **School climate survey**. Many schools participate in this type of survey delivered annually to their community. It's a great way to get to know what is happening.

5. **Community walks**. Parents and students organize community walks to help school staff understand the families they serve. These walks are especially beneficial when there are differences between the teaching staff and the community. The educator and leadership coach Shane Safir is an advocate of community walks; read about her experience in part 4 of this book.

6. **Home visits**. We've already touched on this and we will talk more about it in part 3. Visit kids' homes before school starts and let them know you are excited to see them back at school. On my visits, I have asked parents if there is anything I can do for them. They often say, "You visiting us is enough! Thank you for letting us know you care."

These are just a few ways that you can gain empathy. When you gain empathy, you start to understand what you need to do to serve your community. It's not always easy, but it is very rewarding and worthwhile to take the time to gain that empathy. Take a moment and review the list above. What can you easily do in the next week to gain more empathy for your students or their parents?

Research the research

In education right now, the term "research-based" is thrown around like it is a solution to all our problems. We often think that if an idea is research-based then the results speak for themselves, and so we should adopt it wholesale.

This couldn't be further from the truth. Just because "research shows" that a program in education was effective, that doesn't mean it will be effective in your school, with your students. When it comes to research in scientific studies, there should be a control group and an experimental group. When it comes to any education-related research, there is no control group and every group is experimental. There's no way to judge how the same group of students would have fared had they not been given the same information or same exposure to a program.

I'm certainly not saying that we should take the opposite stance and conclude that educational research doesn't mean anything at all. What we do need to do is take the time necessary to weigh and evaluate any research that is presented to us, and not assume that it is always all it is cracked up to be.

John Hattie's meta-analyses,[10] while valuable and interesting, may be doing an even bigger disservice to schools by abstracting the context and variables in a given study even more. Again, don't misinterpret what I am saying: I don't mean that we should throw the baby out with the bathwater and ignore the good work of Hattie. But, for example, mainstreaming students is good, even though the effect size is low. If we only make decisions based on effect size, we are missing a huge piece of the puzzle. Mainstreaming only had positive results in my school. The students made progress socially and academically, and other students benefited from their presence in class.

So, we shouldn't avoid a policy around mainstreaming students because it has a low effect size. We need to do more than just look at the effect size and then make a snap decision. Nor should we start having students self-report grades just because it has a big effect size. We need to look at how the school is set up and how the policy would impact and be accepted by the community. Then we should do what is right for our school, and do it well.

---

10 John Hattie, *Visible Learning*, Routledge, 2008

In my last district, self-reporting grades would have resulted in all kids getting As because the grades were used as weapons of mass destruction. So much weight was given to grades that self-reporting would have incentivized students to give themselves good grades for no other reason than having good grades.

There is always more to the puzzle than what is reported by a number. Just like there is more to kids or teachers than what is reported by a grade or a rating on an evaluation. For self-reporting grades to be effective, students need a lot more support in other areas. If you don't have standards, and scales aligned to those standards, students won't know what to choose; they will most likely choose to give themselves the grade that will get them in the least trouble when they go home!

So, while Hattie's work is valuable in helping us to understand some things in education, you can't assume that meta-analyses of studies will result in things working out perfectly for your school. By extension, the stories and examples I use in this book won't work exactly for you as they did for me. You have to know your school and community well enough to make decisions that will benefit them.

If we adopt a research-based intervention program for our students, it may actually be more detrimental to our students' success. For example, we adopted a math intervention program at one of my schools. Students in that program showed gains, regularly, but rarely enough to move them out of the program. The teacher who administered (I chose this word carefully) did so with fidelity, and her students were realizing the promised gains, but those gains weren't enough to get them back on grade level. This teacher thrived on routine, on practice, on predictability.

We hired another teacher to do a similar job because our students were really struggling and the caseload was too much for this one intervening teacher. The second teacher, however, could not do that program with fidelity if her life depended on it. You see, while she appreciated routine and deliberate practice, this was not her strength. We structured classes so that she could learn this system from the other teacher and figure out how to make it work for her. Short story: it would never have worked for her. We could have forced it, but I'm so glad we didn't. We would have sucked the life out of that teacher and she would have left the profession.

She needed a different approach. She gave her students the standards and assessments, and told them where they were low; she then taught lessons and used her relationships to inspire those kids to greatness. In just a few short months, we saw that students were ready to leave the intervention program and go back into the regular classroom, regardless of how many grade levels behind they were.

The first teacher's "research-based program" helped students to grow two grade levels in one year. Meanwhile, the second teacher's relationships- and standards-based approach helped students to grow up to four grade levels in a single year.

A note about fidelity. "Fidelity" is the lie we tell ourselves to make the research work. If we do the program exactly how they say we should, then we should get similar results. This is an attempt to have a control group and not an experimental group, and that is impossible. But rather than be concerned about fidelity, let's recognize that all we do in education is in desperate hope for something to work for our students. Sometimes we do amazing things and sometimes we really struggle. That's OK. We are human.

A final word about leadership

Once, when I was talking with a colleague, he was very clear that the school he was leading was not *his* school. He was an employee of the district and could be moved at a moment's notice, and the school would be around long after he was gone.

Another time, one of my curriculum directors told me that it was clear that my school's vision was *my vision*, and there were people in the school who felt they didn't have a place in that vision.

Both of these perspectives are totally valid. Principals should have a vision for their school and it should be their vision. It should, of course, align with the vision of the district, if applicable. It should also be unique to that school. Too often, schools exist that leave a lot to be desired. There is nothing compelling about them. They are just another school. School leaders need to have a vision that is compelling and they need people to buy into that vision.

One district I worked with was rolling out a big initiative to the whole school district. Guess how many people had a "this too shall pass" mentality? A lot. Why? Because they didn't have their own vision of what their school would look like with this initiative. They were waiting for the school district to tell them how they should feel about this new direction.

Well, the district made it pretty clear that this was the direction, and one of the superintendent's cabinet members asked me what I perceived was lacking among the principals. Sadly, it was easy to identify. No principals had any clue what this initiative looked like beyond exactly what the district was saying about it. The principals couldn't see a future where they weren't focusing on something else three years later. And what's worse, they couldn't see how focusing on this right now would lead to focusing on something else as a next evolutionary step!

I suggested that each school create their own vision of what role their school would play in the district initiative. Each school could create that and then they would have a better idea of where to go, while remaining within the boundaries that the district had laid out.

It took a lot of work and a lot of hard conversations to help the principals see what needed to happen. Some got it and others waited for further directives from the district. Those principals who could not make their school identifiable never left a mark on the school community. But those principals who could articulate an individual vision for their school did leave a lasting legacy in their communities.

Furthermore, when the coronavirus closures hit in spring 2020, I saw that the panicked principals were those who were waiting for direction in all things from the district. Whereas the schools that had clear vision were using their time effectively and utilizing people's strengths. They were actually *thriving* during the crisis.

PART 2
The teacher experience

In this section, we're going to think about the experience of the teachers in your school and how you can communicate more effectively with them. Open, honest, clear communication is the solution to so many of the problems that we face in schools. Distorted communication, talking around the problems, and not tackling them head-on can lead to frustration, burnout, and disappointment.

No matter the challenges you face, if your teachers know that they can communicate with you openly about any issue, that will really help to alleviate stress and confusion – and to improve your relationships.

Building trust

One of Stephen Covey's seven habits of highly effective people[11] is "seek first to understand, then to be understood." We need to truly understand our teachers – not only what they are saying, but also what they are feeling, what their motivations are, and how they want and need help.

In her book *Fierce Conversations*,[12] Susan Scott writes of asking a billionaire how he lost his fortune. His response? "Gradually, and then very suddenly." According to Scott, that is also how most relationships end. Have you ever watched a relationship between an employee and boss turn sour? Is there much that can be done to fix it? Not really. Once the trust is broken, it is very difficult to repair.

11 Stephen R. Covey, *The 7 Habits of Highly Effective People*, Free Press, 1989
12 Susan Scott, *Fierce Conversations*, Piatkus, 2017

The educator and author Zaretta Hammond talked to me about our negativity bias, saying that we have a tendency to remember negative situations and hold on to negative things. In order to overcome that, she says, we need to notice and name good things for 30-90 seconds. That is not easy for someone to do on their own.

We must start building trust as early in the employer-employee relationship as we possibly can. If you are hiring someone, you start there. You are inviting them to trust *you* as much as you trust them. I have learned so much about hiring from the educational leadership coach Jimmy Casas. He recognizes that everything is about communication.

When someone applies for a job with Casas, they get a call from him. He greets them and talks about what they are interested in. He sets up the interview himself and makes sure it is scheduled at a time that is convenient for the applicant. Casas says there is no better commodity than time. If you are giving your time to a potential teacher, you are laying the foundations of a positive relationship in which you are there for them.

Casas told me that the purpose of an interview is not to see how a person reacts when caught off-guard, but rather how they behave at their best. That's why he makes sure they feel comfortable. He tells them where to park, where to enter the building, who will be on the interview committee, and anything else they need to know.

You may be wondering how you can find time to do all that when you have five open positions and dozens of people applying for each job. Well, hiring is the single most important thing you do as a principal, so you have to get it right. Casas encourages principals to be involved in every aspect of the hiring process, in order to make sure that you get the best candidate you can. It's that important. He makes it clear to the interview committee that they can make a recommendation, but he doesn't relinquish his authority in having the final say.

His way isn't the only way. Keven Barker, a principal in Arizona, allows his teachers to make the decision. They are the ones who will work with the new hire day in and day out. And they are the ones who will be stuck with the consequences of whatever decision is made. Teachers, Barker told me, are much more honest when someone doesn't fit the culture, and they are much more invested when they find someone they really like. Making them a part of the hiring process helps you to build trust with the people you already have in your school.

Personality types

What happens if you have some challenging relationships, but you can't really start over? You start over anyway. Early on in my podcast interviews, this idea kept coming up. People called it different things, but it ultimately came down to what Covey says about seeking to understand first. This is really hard! In *Fierce Conversations*, Scott states that there are really four people in every conversation:

• The person who is saying something.
• The person who is meaning something.
• The person who is listening.
• The person who is making a different meaning than what was said.

I use the DISC personality test to help me understand my teachers. When we start looking at personality tests, we must realize two things. First, a personality definition or profile will not tell us everything (or at least not completely accurately). People are people and personalities can change. Employees can be wary if they are taking a personality test because their boss has asked them to. They may try to give the "right" answers, as if there were right answers. So don't expect a personality profile to provide all the answers about what makes someone tick.

Second, a personality profile is really a framework for how we can talk about things we don't usually talk about. When you take a personality test, you should understand that it will take time for you to understand it yourself, and you may change in different situations. Nevertheless, personality tests are a valuable tool for helping you to understand your employees better and communicate with them more effectively.

Below is a list of how people with particular personality traits can behave. A disclaimer: this is not an exhaustive list, and one person may identify with all or none of the descriptions. It is important to get to know people personally, but their personality profile can give you a good indication of how to break through the communication barrier.

- **High Dominance**: the High D is characterized by a go-getting attitude and is focused on results more than pretty much anything else. They don't waste a lot of time on getting to know people, but really want to accomplish tasks. The High D can be frustrated, annoyed, or bothered by some of the other personalities.
- **High Influence**: party people! The High I is all about people. What people think and feel about them is very important to them. They will often do things for the sake of attention from others. If you've ever had a class clown, they are likely a High I.
- **High Steadiness**: conflict is super-scary to the High S. They will avoid it at all costs, with students, parents, colleagues, and especially with their boss. They often think they are in trouble if the principal walks through the door.
- **High Compliance**: the High C is characterized by details, details, details. They are reading this right now and asking, "What else?" These are the people who ask lots of questions at every opportunity. If can often seem as if they are finding holes in plans with their questions, and they are. That's what they do. For the High D, this can be very annoying.

In my experiences with multiple staff groups, I have found that many educators are High S and High C. Many administrators are High I and High D. This is important. High D can make High S and High C uncomfortable. Add in the fact that many teachers refer to administration as "the dark side" and principals are in for an uphill battle from the beginning.

Recognizing the various types of personalities is important, especially as it relates to change in our schools. If we have a team full of High S personalities, change is going to be very difficult indeed, because just the idea of change is disagreeable to them, especially if they don't see the need.

We can use personality profiles to make the individual experiences of our staff members the best they can be. If you highlight a High S's achievement in public, they are not going to be happy about that. On the other hand, if you *don't* recognize a High I in front of others, they are going to wonder if you care about them.

	High D	High I	High S	High C
Change	Give me a task and I will make it happen, and can I lead the change?	If people are happy with it, sure.	Uh, no.	What will the change entail? Who will it impact? How will we know it is working? Does the district office support this? What will happen if it fails? Wait, you haven't thought of a plan B yet?
Recognition	Yes, in public, recognizing my valuable contributions to the task.	Yes, in front of everyone. If we could throw a party for me, that would be better.	Yes, in private.	Yes, in private.
Lesson plans	Big picture. Thematic units. Let each day unfold as it may.	Lots of group work, collaboration, and partnering with others.	Lots of detail and many parts planned out.	Extreme levels of detail. Every minute is planned, possibly with contingencies.
Leadership	Yes, I'm ready for it, even if I'm not.	Yes, if it will help me to build relationships, as long as I don't have to make anyone mad at me.	Yes, if there is not conflict. We need to make sure we are all on the same page (may do whatever High D suggests to keep the peace).	What do you mean by leadership? Is the decision already made? What are my boundaries? Who else is on the team? What is the goal? What is the secondary goal?

	High D	High I	High S	High C
Feedback	Direct. To the point. Get right to it.	Could fear that feedback means you don't like them.	Compliment sandwich is necessary. You may need to reaffirm that you still care about the High S and you want to help them.	Provide an opportunity to ask questions about the feedback. If you aren't specific and fail to provide details, they will fight tooth and nail against your feedback.
Faculty meetings	Needs action, tasks, purpose. Wants the meeting to be focused and on point.	Celebrations, chit-chat, lots of interaction. Will be the first to comment in most situations.	Focused on avoiding conflict. Prefers decisions already made. If decisions are already made, they would benefit greatly from a heads-up before the meeting.	Needs time to think about and process the decisions to be made. Provide a heads-up and allow them to ask questions for success.

Recognition and feedback

In a study highlighted in Chip and Dan Heath's book *The Power of Moments*,[13] researchers asked managers how much they recognize their staff. About 80% said they did so regularly or very often. When the employees of those managers were asked, they said 20%. That is a big disparity.

In Daniel Pink's book *When*,[14] he talks about how people like positive endings. What you say in the beginning is critical, but what you say at the end is even more important. If you end on a high note, that is ideal. But this doesn't mean that the "compliment sandwich" approach is the right way to go when it comes to giving recognition and feedback.

---

13 Chip Heath and Dan Heath, *The Power of Moments*, Bantam Press, 2017
14 Daniel H. Pink, *When: the scientific secrets of perfect timing*, Canongate Books, 2018

Justin Baeder, director of the Principal Center, is a master at teaching administrators how to give feedback to teachers. He says that rather than using the compliment sandwich, you should focus on having a powerful conversation with teachers about their instruction, and end on a high note that is respectful of their personality style.

Here's an example. Teacher Courtney is a High D. She is motivated by tasks and by leadership opportunities. She appreciates feedback, but is already so focused on improving herself that a principal coming in and saying, "That was a good questioning sequence you asked" doesn't really cut the mustard for her. She knows it's good. That's why she did it. What she needs is additional responsibilities and the trust to carry those out.

Designing feedback

Let's use our design-thinking process to prototype some approaches to feedback. Choose four teachers in your school that are different from each other. Take a few minutes to think deeply about them. In your experience of working with them, what has made their eyes light up? What has crushed them? What has made them feel embarrassed? Note your reflections in the space below.

1.

2.

3.

4.

Choose one of those teachers and determine how you are going to change your approach with that person specifically. What will you do? Why will you do it differently than you have in the past? This doesn't have to be big. It could something as simple as recognition that they would appreciate. Here are some ideas for what might work according to their personality type.

- **High D**: a brief but sincere thanks, and more responsibility.
- **High I**: a silly award in front of everyone at a faculty meeting (for example, The Golden Flop for a risk they took that didn't really work out).
- **High S**: whatever you do, don't call them down to the office and don't let them feel like they are in trouble.
- **High C**: they need a similar approach to the High S, but make sure that you focus on the details of why things went the way they did. Give your own details and then ask them for their insight on why you are grateful to them.

Now it's time to reflect. How did your interaction go? Did you know the person well enough to see what impact your actions had on them? Did the interaction build or tear down your relationship? And let's iterate: what are you going to do next time to make this easier? In my trainings with principals about personality styles, they often indicate that understanding a teacher's personality style helps the teacher to flourish in ways they have never seen.

Personalized approaches

I'd like to share a story about recognition and validation. I was a principal in a school with a pretty strong and clear district initiative that attracted a lot of criticism from many teachers, community members, and others. I, on the other hand, had come to the school in order to deliver the initiative: personalize learning. I had been trying to do this my entire career. It was exciting to me, but it was very scary to a 19-year veteran teacher. She was a High S and any kind of change alarmed her. She also feared conflict, so if I asked her to do something, she would do it to avoid a confrontation.

Understanding what made her tick made it easier for me to personalize my approach for her. As she dutifully attempted to personalize learning in her classroom, she was always asking if what she was doing was "right." That's a very difficult question for a principal to answer, because the proof is in the pudding – with the kids. So, she knows the answer better than I do. But she was looking for validation, as a High S is wont to do.

As I discussed her strategies and plans with her (and she really was trying her best), she didn't need me to solve any problems for her. She needed to talk through them and make sure that her ideas were "right" in my eyes. She made some mistakes and those were celebrated, because she was afraid that she was failing. I assured her that she wasn't. She was also a fairly High C, so she knew her issues inside and out – all she needed from me was validation.

As you're reading this, you might think, "Well, that's what all our teachers need." And you're right! They need validation in ways that are *personalized* for them. We need to lean in to each teacher's preferred style, to make sure that our communication is clear and they get what they need to be successful.

What's your storyline?

Communication cards (find them at schoolx.me/cards) are very powerful conversation starters. They allow you to define what the conversation is going to be about. Has someone ever come to you to complain about something and you try to solve the problem, but they don't want that? Or have you ever had someone drop a huge problem on your desk and expect you to solve it? That's what a communication card can help with.

There are seven communication cards:

- I need to vent.
- I need help solving a problem.
- It's all about the money.
- I have a problem in my personal life.
- I want to brag.
- I made a mistake.
- I have a storyline.

Most of those are pretty self-explanatory, but the one I want to focus on here is "I have a storyline." When it comes to communication, everyone has a storyline. A storyline is where you have a *perspective* about what someone else feels, but you tell yourself that your perspective is the truth. Let's say you are in a board meeting and the superintendent gives you a look. You know the one: it's not a smiling face. An eyebrow is raised. You start thinking about something that you did recently, and you connect the look and the conversation to what you did, and you start to feel like this is all your fault and you think you are in trouble with your boss. Then you're afraid to talk to her about it. It starts eating at you, keeping you up at night, and you make a concerted effort to stay under the radar.

You tell yourself a story based on a look, but you have no idea whether or not that story is actually true. But now that you've told yourself this story, you can't believe anything other than that. You're not going to bring it up, but you're sick about it.

When teachers use the storyline card with me, I make it a point to be free of judgement, to be patient, and to let them express everything they need to. Then I commit to being honest about what I meant by that look. When people think they are in trouble, 99% of the time they really aren't. This is especially the case with people who are High S, who often believe there is conflict even when there is not.

The real power of communication cards is that they give people who might usually avoid confrontation a way to address an issue. They give a voice to those who don't often use their voice. As I was leaving one school to join another, a teacher said to me, "If you don't take anything else with you, make sure you use the communication cards. These have made it so much easier to talk with you."

That comment helped me to realize how powerful communication cards are. I had a number of difficult conversations with this teacher that just would not have happened without them.

Support v accountability

Teachers often say they want to be supported. Administrators often say they need to hold teachers accountable. When teachers want support, sometimes that means, "The principal should do what I want them to."

As leaders, we know that what we want is sometimes not the best thing for us. We also understand that it is incumbent on us to help everyone in our organization to show growth. We are either growing or we are dying. There is no stasis.

Sometimes support looks more like accountability and sometimes it looks like doing what teachers want. I once worked with a teacher who had a student who was being a real pill in class. This teacher and I had talked many times about the need for our school to be less about control and more about empowerment. So, when the teacher came to me and said that he was ready to pin that kid to the wall because of his misbehavior, I responded with, "It sounds like you want to exert your control over him." He said, "Yes, I think I do." I invited him to choose a path that didn't involve exerting control over the student. How could he invite the student to make a better choice? That was my challenge for him.

With that kind of support, he changed his game and approached the student in a respectful, solution-focused way. Later, he said to me, "How did you get me to work so hard?" Well, we reached that point together because we both worked on communicating effectively.

Supporting teachers is vitally important. But it doesn't always look how they want it to look. I had another teacher whose students had plagiarized content. She wanted the students suspended. When I declined to assign that as the punishment, she expressed the view that I didn't support teachers and teachers shouldn't bother sending kids to me. Although I agreed with the idea that teachers have the most power when they solve their own problems, it's not true that the only way a principal can show support is by implementing the suggested consequences. I certainly did support her by talking to those students and helping them to see that plagiarism is wrong.

Invigorating your teachers

In his book *Future Focused Leaders*,[15] Dr. Bill Ziegler lists three things that a school leader needs to do to be ultimately successful: relate, innovate, invigorate.

---

15 Bill Ziegler and Dave Ramage, *Future Focused Leaders*, Corwin Press, 2017

I want to talk about the "invigorate" part of that approach. Invigorate, according to Ziegler, means that you inspire people to remember their original motivation to become a teacher. One of the benefits of working in education is that you and your colleagues mostly got into it for the same reason and are probably still in it for the same reason: you care about kids' success in life. That doesn't mean that it isn't hard. So many of the communication challenges that we face exist because our system can stand in the way of us doing amazing things with kids.

A teacher who is not invigorated is probably a teacher who is burned out. It's easy to burn out in this system, but we can't let that happen.

This is where the design-thinking process can really be beneficial. You, as the leader, get to work with teachers on this. Talk with them about what they are missing in their job. Find a way to empathize with how that is impacting on kids. Then work with the teacher to come up with ways to overcome those impacts on students. Implement those ideas, reflect, and come up with something else to make things better. Let's walk through this process with a specific example.

We'll call the teacher Mrs. Johnson. She's an experienced teacher who has been there, done that, and is increasingly frustrated that the kids just aren't how they used to be. She loves them and she works hard, but the work is getting harder and harder.

In an interview, I ask her what is challenging and what are the missteps that make her frustrated. We talk about the pressures from me, her principal, to do certain things. This is an important step, because the principal has the power to change things – not everything, but some things, and certainly in the short-term. Mrs. Johnson is frustrated that she has to change the attendance record for students who are late, so we decide that she doesn't need to take attendance until 10 minutes into class. Then we realize that she'll never stop in the middle of a lesson to take attendance, and decide that taking attendance at the end of class is suitable. I take off her plate what I can take off.

We use a protocol called dialogical interviews, which I learned from Eric Chagala, principal of Vista Innovation and Design Academy in California. Dialogical interviews are a way to gain empathy. I ask Mrs. Johnson the following questions:

- What was your life like growing up?
- What were your schooling experiences like growing up?
- Why did you become an educator?
- Why are you still in education?
- What gets you up in the morning?
- What keeps you up at night?
- Has there ever been a moment in your life when your assumptions about someone were disproven? What happened? How did that moment impact your thinking?
- What masks do you wear?
- How do masks help us?
- How do they hurt us?

These questions help me to understand her better and help her to open up. Mrs. Johnson laments that her students don't seem to be having as much fun as her previous students did. That makes it hard for her to have fun. We talk about what made learning fun before and what is making it not fun today. She talks about how the kids are more unruly, so she doesn't trust herself to do more fun things with them because she's afraid that she will lose control and there will be chaos. We talk about her expectations and how she communicates them to students. We talk about how her students feel towards the expectations she has. I ask her to imagine she is one of her most well-behaved students and what that experience is like. Then to imagine she is one of her worst-behaved students. It's hard for her to put herself in their shoes because she has already judged them to be a certain way, but we try anyway.

John is, of course, a good student because his mom is a teacher in another school and Mrs. Johnson knows her personally. John works hard and does everything he needs to, right away. That's great for Mrs. Johnson, but she identifies that he feels frustrated because other students are making bad choices and he often feels the consequences of their behavior. He has expressed frustration to his mom about that and she has let Mrs. Johnson know. Mrs. Johnson believes that John's day is also frustrating for him because of other issues.

Susie's mom is also a teacher, but Susie can't sit in her seat for 30 seconds without being distracted. She wants to touch and feel everything. Mrs. Johnson doesn't know Susie's mom, but she doesn't think Susie's mom can be a very good teacher, because of Susie's behavior. Mrs. Johnson tries to empathize with Susie, but has a very hard time. She works it out as best she can and concludes that Susie is overstimulated, with too many things happening in the classroom.

We agree that Mrs. Johnson needs to have some conversations with these two kids to see what is going on. We generate a list of questions for her to ask, much like the questions I asked her, to help her gain empathy with the students.

- What do you do for fun at home?
- What has school been like for you?
- Who was your best teacher so far?
- Why were they your best teacher?
- Why are you excited to come to school?
- What bothers you about school?

Mrs. Johnson realizes that she needs to know this about all her students, but she wants to start with these two students. After a few days she finds the time to meet with them, and later we discuss what she has learned. She finds it fascinating that the students have had the same teachers before and have come away with completely different experiences. One commonality is that they both enjoyed a teacher who did lots of hands-on things. Susie liked that teacher because she didn't get in trouble as much; she worked hard to be a class leader in the activities. John liked that teacher because he felt like the time in school went by quicker.

Although it was difficult to find time for those conversations, just having them invigorates Mrs. Johnson. She wants to try a prototype where Susie can earn a hands-on activity, but she has no idea how to fit it into the curriculum. She knows there needs to be a purpose. We talk about how to make that happen and simple ways to track it. She thinks a "warm fuzzy" jar for Susie will be most beneficial: each time Susie follows directions the first time she is asked, she has a warm fuzzy placed on her desk. But when Mrs. Johnson implements this, the warm fuzzy acts as a distraction and ends up getting thrown around the room. Time to iterate!

In the meantime, I invite Mrs. Johnson to observe some other teachers who are doing cool things with their kids. Recognizing that she can't be a different teacher, and knowing that she needs to focus her energies on things she is comfortable with, she takes a couple of ideas from each teacher and starts making plans for more hands-on activities in her class.

Mrs. Johnson decides that the warm fuzzies need to stay on the desk! She creates a story about a warm-fuzzy village that is on a high mountain with cliffs all around it. Susie loves the story; she starts naming her warm fuzzies and giving them background stories. She is careful that they don't fall off the desk, but when one inevitably does, Mrs. Johnson and Susie have a moment of silence for their fallen comrade and a quick lesson about staying away from the edges of the cliffs.

Amazingly, Mrs. Johnson sees that this "audience" makes it even easier for Susie to be where she is supposed to be and do what she is supposed to do. She quickly earns enough warm fuzzies for a hands-on activity. Through her dialogical interviews with the rest of her students, Mrs. Johnson had learned that many of them would benefit from hands-on activities and she had already implemented them. But, to be true to her word, she made a special activity for the class when Susie got enough warm fuzzies.

In this example, you can see that it takes time to get somewhere. Mrs. Johnson had to work for things to be the best they could. This is a process. Don't forget that.

But in seeking success with those two students, she made things better for all her students. Not only that, but she also started to remember why she got into teaching in the first place. She saw with fresh eyes why she needed to be there for the kids and what joy they brought her.

Learning from colleagues

Ziegler suggests that we provide job-embedded professional development for our teachers. That means that instead of pulling them out of the building, sending them to an all-day training session, and then not having any follow-up, we work with them one-on-one or one-on-a-few to help them be successful. We focus on the things they actually need to improve.

We started this at my school when we saw that teachers wanted to learn from each other. We knew we didn't want to have another evaluation or observation with accountability from yet another person. So, we asked teachers what they wanted to learn from their peers and set up a structure for a fun activity.

The idea came from our personalized learning team meeting, where we were brainstorming ways to show teachers what the personalized learning team had gained by doing learning walks in each other's classrooms. As we talked, we followed the design-thinking process and tried to figure out, as best we could, what would feel like a directive and what would feel like it was a fun thing to be involved with. We sought empathy by asking how we would feel if we were in their position and we received this information from us.

When we first started talking about the idea, it was really about how we could make the other teachers participate, with the message coming from administration. We quickly realized that was not the right approach and we should instead let the personalized learning team do the communicating about the learning-walk opportunity, because they knew how powerful it had been for them.

Next we considered accountability. We knew that no accountability would lead to nobody doing the learning walks. Some accountability would be yet another thing for us (administration) to track. A lot of accountability, with observation forms and so on, would be a nightmare and nobody would enjoy it.

After discussing how teachers might feel about different approaches, ranging from simple Google forms to actual observation forms to fill out ad nauseam, we decided on a prototype contest to see which teacher could visit the most classrooms, and who could be visited the most – the Curious Colleague Challenge. The name avoided the word "observation" and seemed a pretty non-threatening, fun way to approach the situation. As it turns out, people like to not feel threatened!

We wanted people to feel like they had something to share with their fellow teachers, and to know that they could learn something, too. We also wanted them to know that they didn't have do anything fancy when they had a visit, nor when they visited. We decided that teachers needed to answer three questions:

1. Do you want your Curious Colleagues to drop in or schedule an appointment?
2. What is the #1 strength of your classroom?
3. What do you want to see from your colleagues? (With checkboxes for personalized learning, teaching strategies, classroom management, classroom design, flexible content, student reflection and ownership, gathering and use of qualitative and quantitative data, targeted instruction.)

We had a much different survey planned in our heads, but once we got our initial prototype laid out, we knew we had to do something else. We iterated, adjusting our plan as necessary to meet the needs of our teachers. Now, outside of each classroom is a QR code that takes teachers to a Google form to capture their learning. There are four short questions:

1. Curious Colleague's name.
2. Visited teacher's name.
3. How long did you learn in their classroom?
4. What did you learn from being there?

It takes teachers just a few seconds to record their experience and then we have some fun data. We take the time teachers spend observing and add it to our running leaderboard, which is updated in the office about once a month. And we throw in prizes occasionally to get people more excited about the process.

Preparing for hard conversations

The wind howled as I walked to work that day. It was almost as though the wind knew what was in my heart and was pushing me to go back home. I was dreading the hard conversation I needed to have. I had already laid the groundwork, subtly telling the teacher that he would not be welcomed back to our school next year. But today, I needed to have the bigger conversation. It needed to be clear; there could be no ambiguity.

I felt like a failure.

Frank had done wonderful work in his previous district, helping kids to increase their scores significantly, but he was so rude to our students. I thought of the students who had been harmed because of Frank's actions. I knew it was worth my discomfort to make sure kids knew they were going to be safe (emotionally and physically) while at school.

I reflected on what Jennifer Abrams had told me about the four key questions to ask before a hard conversation.

1. **Is this a hard conversation or a clarifying conversation?** "We think we have been clear," Abrams says. "So, it makes sense that we should be able to speak up and express our concern, but…warning. Take pause. Did we actually make it clear from the get-go what is and isn't part of the job or task?"

Did Frank know that his behavior was not acceptable? Had I talked with him enough for him to know that his behavior would result in him not being able to come back to our school? I was affecting his livelihood and that is a big deal to me. We had met at numerous times throughout the year and I had said certain things that I had thought made it clear, but sometimes those things don't seem clear enough in hindsight.

I thought about a particular conversation where Frank had flippantly said, "You can't do anything to me because their scores are so high!" I knew that the scores of his students were important and, yes, he was teaching them lots of skills, but we were a trauma-informed school and we did lots of training on how to treat students with respect. When he held grades over their heads like carrots on a stick, they achieved, but I worried that it exposed them to more traumatic experiences than they needed.

When I told him that the scores were not the most important thing in the world, he was shocked. He completely believed that demeaning students was worth it if their scores were high enough. We had been through that enough times over the year – he should have understood. This was a hard conversation, not a clarifying conversation.

2. **Can I articulate the problem in a professional way that is tied to job descriptions?** "Saliva moments happen. I often made them happen," Abrams says. "A saliva moment is when something is said too pointedly; it is too generalized and too opinionated. The other person grimaces, sucks in a breath and saliva is heard. It is the moment of the 'too harsh' statement."

I'd had many saliva moments with Frank. One time, when I confronted him about a situation where he had generalized a student's behavior because of his race, I said, "You can't blame his race for your inability to connect with him." There was definitely saliva there! I was shocked by his behavior. His negative behavior extended to other staff members as well and he couldn't connect with his team. There were, of course, other times when he did great things.

Abrams says, "When we get frustrated, we go emotional with our language. 'Too' or 'very.' 'Always' or 'never' – adverbs that inflame. Do I know how to say what I want to say but in a professional way? And can it be tied to the language of the job description? The standards? The expectations?"

I thought about how to approach this situation. Frank didn't care about his students and he didn't support them, especially kids with special needs, who he said didn't belong in his class until they were on grade level (because they would bring down his scores). I knew that if I had another saliva moment in this conversation, he would push back hard.

My plan was to use contract language. But, knowing that Frank would push back, I would need to cite examples and clarify why his behavior was bad enough to warrant the non-renewal of his contract, even though he did achieve growth in his students. I needed to point to specific standards of professional behavior, like including all students, using appropriate language in front of students, and not exposing them to inappropriate material in school.

The wind whipped me as I rounded a corner. The rain began. Although I knew I was about to do the right thing, my approach seemed as unclear as my path to work through my rain-speckled glasses.

3. **Do I have an answer to "What do you want me to do about it?"**
Abrams says, "It is understandable to be frustrated, but at this moment in time, the person is looking for some takeaways and you want to see a different behavior. They want to get a more specific sense of what the actions should be to have you see them as effective in their role, and it is a humane and growth-producing thing to do to have a few answers at the ready that are doable. Consider the frustration they might feel when they are told they aren't collaborating effectively, and yet the person sharing this with them can't describe one action they could take. Many times we are too broad with our suggestions."

Did I want to see a behavior change from Frank? Yes, but did it matter at this point? Would it save his job? Was he too far gone? Had I let things go on too long? Should I have had this conversation months ago? Furthermore, when do I switch from being the supportive coach to the disciplinarian administrator who has to make a difficult decision and have that hard conversation? These questions tormented me as the wind and rain chilled me to the bone.

I *had* spoken to Frank on previous occasions. I had been supportive. I had helped him to find ways to overcome his challenges. I had invited him to observe other teachers, and given him opportunities to take coaching and additional classes. If he were to ask, "What do you want me to do about it?", what would I say?

I resolved that I would say, "You need to listen to what students are saying before you react to what they did. Rather than jump down their throats, you need to let them express themselves." Even as I thought it, I knew that he wouldn't be able to do such a thing. More importantly, the kids had learned that he wouldn't listen to them and they had given up.

This question really scared me. How would I react if he begged to keep his job? How would I react if he begged to be given one more chance?

I knew that this had to be the end. If he asked, "What do you want me to do about it?", my answer had to be, "There's nothing more to do. This is a final decision."

Oh, the pain! I didn't want to fire someone! I believe in giving people chances, training, and opportunities to overcome their weaknesses. I want them to be successful, but it was time this situation came to a head.

Previously, I had given Frank examples of what he could do to make things better for himself and his students. He would try them a couple of times, but then go back to his old ways. It was so difficult to keep reminding him about his negative behavior and the possible consequences.

I had an obligation to support this teacher professionally. If he could be successful as a teacher somewhere else, I wanted him to move on.

4. Have I been too suggestive in my language when I need to be more direct? This question hit me hard. I want to be a coaching principal, not a directive or heavy-handed principal. I want the coaching relationship to last as long as possible, because when that relationship exists, it is really amazing.

Abrams says, "Baby boomers have traditionally been known for having hard conversations in very diplomatic ways. Asking folks to 'consider,' or telling them 'just something to think about when you have time' or 'just a thought to keep in mind' when what one really means is DO IT, is read by some of the other generations as too fuzzy or even a bit passive-aggressive. Many boomers are just being kind in their approach and expect you to appreciate the suggestiveness of the language but still get the hint. Not all generations read between the lines in this way. If you have an expectation, a non-negotiable, a must, a 'this is how we do things here,' state it clearly. It isn't mean or too blunt to be clear in one's expectations. Xers and millennials will thank you, and the hard conversation you won't need to have as a result of your clarity will make you thankful, too."

This was not a baby-boomer problem. I reflected on my own language over the year and I knew there was much to improve in my future communications. I hadn't always said things as directly as I should have, but I wasn't *too* suggestive. This was going to be a really hard conversation. My desire to be liked was strong and sometimes I could say things in a way that left teachers unclear about what I really meant. This time, I needed to be directive. This would not be a suggestion. This would not be a relaxed conversation. It would be a confrontation.

As I walked up to the doors of the school, the chill from the wind and the rain seemed to dissipate. I had planned my conversation and reflected on previous conversations. Frank was a good man who wasn't a fit for our school and our students. He had skills, I could give him that, but he wouldn't be at our school the next year. A ray of sunshine appeared through the clouds. I stepped into the school, resolved to have a positive but clear conversation with Frank and his union accompaniment.

As we sat down at the table, I knew the time was right. He was not happy. I felt terrible telling him that he would not be at our school next year, but I also felt *ready* to tell him that because of my preparation.

Having hard conversations is not something that we talk about very much in schools. We rarely relive and share these moments because they are challenging, painful, and awkward. Most importantly, we want to protect the privacy of those we have had hard conversations with. For the record, I changed the name of this teacher, but his story is one that we often hear in education. I include it here not to shame him, but to share an experience of mine that really was challenging.

I once asked one of my mentors, a superintendent, what he would have changed for himself. He said one thing that would have saved him a lot of negative press, embarrassment, and distraction was having an "axe man."

He explained that when you are the leader of an organization, you can get away with being directive and totalitarian if you are always that way. But it's very hard to be a coach and a fiercely critical leader at the same time. Instead of having those intense stand-offs with employees, he wished he had asked one of his assistant superintendents to have the difficult conversations. Sometimes, depending on our skills and leadership styles, an "axe man" can be a good thing to have.

Recently, I made a mistake and my superintendent sent her assistant superintendent to make sure it was clear that I needed to change my behavior. Rather than being offensive, this assistant superintendent and I were able to work through my mistake and make it right.

But most principals are alone and don't have someone to delegate the hard conversations to. You need to be both coach and accountability partner for your staff. In these situations, focusing on clear, honest communication and reviewing these four questions from Jennifer Abrams will help you to save face and be more confident in your decisions.

Teacher guilt

Guilt is something that afflicts every educator at some point in their career. Teachers grew up and were trained in a system that set them up to believe certain things about education, so when teachers do something that is not traditional, they feel like they are not doing what good teachers "should" do.

The best way to illustrate this is by giving a couple of examples.

First, a school district adopts a curriculum and books that are not a good choice for kids. Let's say, for sake of the argument, that they are racially biased, include few multicultural voices, and the content is too challenging for students. Even though Mrs. Jones knows that this curriculum is not a good match for her high-poverty, multicultural class, she still goes back to the book again and again for her lessons, because she "has to follow the curriculum." This is intentionally an extreme example, because most educators today understand that they need to supplement the curriculum, at the very least.

One district I worked with adopted a math curriculum that contained lots of errors, taught advanced concepts before foundational concepts, and had many typos that hindered the work of the children. The math teacher consistently said, "This book is no good and I don't like using it." But he still used it, because it was the adopted curriculum. You see, he couldn't overcome his teacher guilt and do the right thing.

Here's another example. I've talked with many teachers who want to do innovative things in their classrooms, but they are worried about the innovation parts taking too long, and not being able to cover all the content. It's better if they are looking at standards rather than content, but the challenge still remains. "I'd like to engage my students in a project about how government works," a teacher might say, "but I need to cover the Civil War." They feel a pressure to accomplish everything, but they know they don't have enough time, and so they feel guilty about it.

What are some other aspects of teacher guilt that you see?

Removing the obstacles

Mrs. Smith sat in my office, tears filling her eyes and running down her cheeks. "I try so hard," she said. "It seems like all that I do is never good enough. I create the most amazing lessons for my students and I still feel like I am barely holding it all together. I'm barely getting an A in my master's classes. And don't even get me started on the mandated trainings that I still haven't watched."

Mrs. Smith was one of my best teachers. But she suffered from what many of our best teachers suffer from: she thought that everything had the exact same importance. She thought turning in lesson plans to me and watching the trainings mandated by the state and district were as important as meeting her students' needs every day.

We were just starting an evaluation meeting, where she would get even more tasks to do to show evidence of her effectiveness as a teacher. But she was overwhelmed and our conversation that day never got to the evaluation. She needed to vent and she needed help prioritizing.

Many teachers are in the profession because they were successful in the school system. They got good grades and completed all the tasks required of them. But they still struggle with the idea that they need to make others happy by doing what they are told. They also suffer from the tragic mindset that they have to do everything perfectly.

So, let's talk about how to support those teachers who have so much on their plate. My purpose over the next few pages is to help you remove all obstacles in front of teachers.

Empathy

Before you can really start removing obstacles, you need have an understanding of what teachers are going through. Chris Horton, a principal in British Columbia, Canada, uses cognitive coaching for this. The only statements he makes when coaching teachers are paraphrases of what he understands the teacher to be saying. Otherwise, it is all questions. This approach makes it easier to learn what is truly going on in the teacher's head and to find ways to support her.

The goal of cognitive coaching is for the teacher to achieve a shift in her thinking. There are three aspects to remember to make it effective. First, you must ask questions and allow the person to make the statements that work for them, not for you. Horton offers some solid advice: "Don't mind the rabbit trails, because the rabbit trail could be meaningful to that person." Your questions should be phrased to elicit deeper thought and truth, not to take the coaching where you want it to go.

We are trying to figure out what a teacher has on her plate, so we can remove some of it. The reason we need to ask questions about this is because we need to understand whether what she is doing is imposed by us, or by someone else, or by herself. So, when we ask about lesson planning and other aspects, we want to find out where the expectations are coming from.

Second, you must listen and ask open-ended questions. One of the key skills you must employ is active listening. Paraphrasing back to the other person is not just a strategy that good listeners use, but is also a way to make sure that what they are saying is what you are *hearing*. As we learned earlier from Susan Scott, there are more than two people in every conversation. It is vital to make sure that we truly understand where people are coming from and what they are intending to say.

Third, you must be curious. When it comes to cognitive coaching, Horton suggests using curiosity about the situation to extend the conversation. One effective strategy is the "five whys," in which you ask the person "why?" five times until you get to the root of the issue. Kindergarten teachers will joke that this strategy is employed by five-year-olds all the time, though not with the same intent that we might have.

Secondary to this stage of empathy-gaining is taking a hard look at what we are asking of teachers. We need to think about what we require, what the district requires, and what the state requires, and make choices that support our ultimate goal of educating children in a powerful way. If you don't know what your vision for education is, it might be wise to go back to part 1 and take some time to work on that, because once you know what you are going for, it becomes easier to take other things off teachers' plates.

For example, my vision is: what is needed, when it's needed. That includes being prepared, which means good lesson plans. But do I need to see those lesson plans, as the principal? No. Do they need to be in a specific format? No. Do they need to be done by Monday morning? The lesson plans for Monday do! Should I make teachers jump through hoops to turn them in, when giving kids what they need when they need it will inevitably lead to lesson plans being changed mid-week, or even mid-lesson? Not at all.

Make a list of the things that are required of your teachers. That will help you to see just how much you are asking of them.

Prototype

Once we have figured out what our teachers are really dealing with, we can start the process of removing some things from their plates. We need to ask two questions:

1. Will removing this make my teacher's life easier or more difficult? If the answer is the latter, then don't remove it.
2. If I can't remove this thing, can I at least make it more manageable or relevant?

In this prototype stage, find an obstacle that you can remove or make more relevant for your teachers. Some ideas will follow. If you change something, you may have a difficult time changing it back, so exercise caution. If you're nervous about changing something required by the district, I strongly suggest that you take the time to talk to your district leadership. It is also important to point out that this is not your burden to carry alone. Many teachers will gladly jump on board if they believe that you are going to make their lives easier. The short-term effort for them will be well worth it if it saves them heaps of time in the long-term.

Now, let's look at some of the areas where you might be able to remove some obstacles for your teachers.

1. Teacher evaluation

Although there have been some improvements in teacher evaluation in the past few years, with states and districts creating their own processes or adopting modern systems from Charlotte Danielson or Robert Marzano, there are still aspects of many of those systems that are burdensome or unnecessary. Look at your system and determine where you can make it easier to accomplish the purpose of evaluation.

I talked a little about Dr. Joe Sanfelippo in the introduction to this book. He is a superintendent in Fall Creek, Wisconsin. Most people don't associate Fall Creek with educational innovation, but those who know Sanfelippo sure do! He was unsatisfied with the teacher evaluation process in his district, so he did something crazy: he changed it.

Sanfelippo told me that although he needs teachers to get better, he doesn't care *how* they get better. As a strengths-based leader, he knows that people who are working in their strengths are happier, more fulfilled, and do better work than those made to feel helpless and hopeless by having to work in their weaknesses. So, Sanfelippo gathered six teachers together and told them, "It's not my journey, it's yours!" He asked them to build a new evaluation process. He placed an extra burden on those teachers for a time, but in a way that would lead to a much better long-term experience for all teachers.

Sanfelippo told his teachers, "Start with passion, we can figure out how to measure it later." The teachers are able to do whatever they want that shows they are growing in some areas. Sanfelippo concedes that only some teachers choose to work on an area of their weakness rather than an area of strength. But he recognizes that those teachers who *choose* to work on an area of weakness are much better positioned to actually improve than those teachers who are forced by administration to address an area where they are struggling.

According to Sanfelippo, "the emotional connection of being in charge of your learning has powerful consequences" – and not just for students. He took his teachers on a journey of evaluation that was about growth in an area of the teacher's choosing. This made everything they did that was related to evaluation much more worthwhile. For his teachers, gone are the days of collecting "evidence" in a binder that will soon be forgotten.

One of the things that we did at my school was to create a blog where teachers could post evidence. At the very least, they would be sharing their evidence with others who could also benefit. What processes do you have in place that could be refined, eliminated, or delayed to make your teacher evaluation system simpler or more manageable?

2. Lesson plans

As a teacher, I never worked at a school where I had to turn in lesson plans. And as a principal, I've never required it of my teachers, because that does not meet with my goals of being an effective principal, but my district has. Some schools expect teachers to submit lesson plans in a specific way. But the person who knows best what the lesson plans should look like is the teacher in the classroom.

Although my district required lesson plans, I told teachers to submit them in whatever format was actually meaningful to them. If the lesson plans they turned in to me were set up in a way that *I* wanted, that would be a waste of their time. I didn't come to education through a teacher preparation program, so I didn't get many lessons myself in creating lesson plans and I don't have a "way" that I want everyone to conform to. I designed my own lesson plans so that the kids could know what was expected and accomplish the work without any help. The reason I designed them that way was so that students who were absent would be able to do the work. That took a considerable amount of effort for me and I believe that it was worth it, because the kids always knew that if they weren't in class, they would miss out socially, but not educationally.

What processes do you have in place around lesson plans? What can be reduced or made easier so that your teachers can meet the needs, but not waste time, effort, or energy on something that doesn't matter?

3. Meetings

There is a great book called *Meetings Suck* by Cameron Herold.[16] Most people can agree with that sentiment! Many principals I have worked with have argued that if it can be said in an email, it shouldn't be said in a faculty meeting.

In the book, Herold writes, "While email is a helpful technology, it can't replace the power of face-to-face communication. Written communication is a minefield of misunderstandings. Consider the sentence, 'I didn't say you were beautiful.' You can interpret that six

---

16 Cameron Herold, *Meetings Suck*, Lioncrest Publishing, 2016

ways depending on which word you emphasize! Six words, six different meanings – and matters only get murkier with more complexity."

Things can also be interpreted differently in meetings. Thus, it is important to know who should actually be in the meeting. "You can save a significant amount of time by having a proper agenda and allowing your people to opt in or out of meetings to which they don't feel they can add value," writes Herold. In one of my schools, the leadership team had regular meetings and, after reading Herold's book, I allowed people to come and go as needed. It meant that I was focused on getting an agenda out early, and giving people time to digest it so that we could have the right people in the room. We even got to the point where we set the agenda for the next meeting at the end of the current meeting.

Then, as Herold writes, some great things happened: "When people make these choices, we should cheer them for their decision to stay focused on their responsibilities and priorities instead of becoming involved in everything. They're looking through the lens of how best to generate value for the [school] through their time and resources, and this is exactly what we want to encourage all our people to do. Plus, when people opt out who don't believe they can provide value, then only those who do believe they can provide value will sit around the table to engage in a more focused discussion."

Herold also states, "No agenda, no attenda!" When we have an agenda with the right people around the table, everyone instantly feels better about the whole meeting.

I'm sure we have all walked out of a meeting and realized that we could have used that time much more effectively doing nearly anything else! When our teachers feel that way about our meetings, it can certainly hurt. So we must work to make sure that all our meetings are as effective as possible. One person quipped to me many years ago, "The worst meeting is one that should have been cancelled but wasn't. The best meeting is one that has been cancelled."

The author and entrepreneur Seth Godin has described the notion of "crisp" meetings. He says, "If it's not going to be a crisp meeting, the professional is well-advised to not even attend." But what is a crisp meeting? It is a meeting that is purposeful and intentional. In his blog post on the subject,[17] Godin presents many questions to ask yourself about meetings. I offer a few below.

- Who should be in the room? (And I would add: does everyone need to attend every faculty meeting?)
- What's the advance preparation that we ought to engage in?
- When things go wrong, what's our approach to fixing them?
- Is everyone in the room enrolled in the same project, or is part of the meeting to persuade the naysayers?

Answering these questions and expecting the preparation work to be done are both very important. The onus is on us to lead meetings in a way that empowers and supports our teachers in their growth and development.

4. Professional development

Dr. Amy Fast, principal at McMinnville High School in Oregon, believes the biggest problem in education is a "culture of top-down leadership and accountability." Although leaders exist for a reason, not everything should come from them. While Fast and her team didn't have the ability to change their evaluation system like superintendent Joe Sanfelippo did, they did have the power to change how they delivered professional development to their large staff.

Like Sanfelippo, they found a common ground in helping teachers to identify their own passions and using professional development time in a manner that would give teachers the chance to develop and deepen their passions.

Rather than talk about having everyone on the same bus, Fast describes the challenge of going from good to great as "each teacher has their own bus, and they're all going in the same direction." The vision shows teachers the direction in which to head, but each individual can take their own bus and their own path to get there.

McMinnville High School uses an embedded professional development model, using lab classrooms. There are three cycles: instruction,

---

17 Seth Godin, "The Crisp Meeting," *Seth's Blog*, 2017, seths.blog/2017/09/the-crisp-meeting

volunteer to try the strategy, and debrief. Teachers will discuss a new way of doing something and one will volunteer to try this new strategy in her classroom. Other teachers will be able to visit her classroom to see how she has managed this new approach, and they will all have an opportunity to discuss this after the lesson. Administrators do drop-ins to provide feedback and add to the discussion, but teachers are leading the charge themselves.

Teachers use those opportunities throughout the year to assess themselves on their growth for their evaluation. According to Fast, the teachers are much harder on themselves than the administration is. She told me, "If you honor the teacher's educational philosophy, you will be able to use their strength to make them even better."

5. Grades and feedback

Students need feedback. They don't really need grades. But the grades are not the part that actually takes a lot of time. Mike Kelly, a principal in Pennsylvania, has been working on this path for many years. In his school, one of his first steps was to remove all notion of time being the constant. He started by moving marking periods from quarters to semesters. He then removed them for an entire school year. The only marking period was at the end of the year.

Taking this burden off teachers completely is a big philosophical shift that has many implications, and we will talk more about it in part 3. Here, what I want to emphasize is that grades reduce a student's learning and skills to a single letter in most cases. It is challenging at best to summarize all the effort that goes into teaching and learning in a single letter. It is downright wrong in most cases. Giving teachers the ability to focus on feedback will relieve many of their other burdens, including parent complaints, phone calls, and meetings about student grades.

One of my biggest frustrations in my first year of teaching was that I would write feedback on student papers, only for them to search for the grade and then dump the paper in the trash can. I learned two things from this:

1. Kids don't care about my feedback.
2. Students only care about their actual grade.

But both of these are false. Kids *do* care about feedback, but they have learned that the only things that "matter" are those that get graded. We've set them up for failure.

Jennifer Gonzalez's *Cult of Pedagogy* blog has a guest post from Kristy Louden that offers a solution to this very problem.[18] Louden suggests that teachers give feedback on the assignment and return that to the students, but don't give them the grade associated with that feedback – yet. Wait a day or two before they see the grade.

Louden writes, "The simple act of delaying the grade meant that students had to think about their writing. They had to read their own writing – after a few weeks away from it – and digest my comments, which allowed them to better recognize what they did well or not so well. The response from students was extremely positive; they understood the benefit of rereading their essays and paying attention to feedback. One boy said, 'Mrs. Louden, you're a genius. I've never read what a teacher writes on my essay before, and now I have to.'"

This approach doesn't eliminate the hard work that a teacher does, but it does give more meaning to that work, because the students actually recognize and pay attention to the feedback.

6. Committees

Do teacher committees exist to provide critical feedback about next steps, or to give the illusion of teachers doing additional important work? I had one teacher say, "I gave up on committees a couple of years back, because it was always a waste of time. The leadership would gather us together to say that we are going to talk about something, but then would have already made the decision."

Take a look at the committees that your teachers are on. In order for them to be successful, they should be action-oriented. Otherwise, you are wasting a lot of time and effort.

---

18 Kristy Louden, "Delaying the Grade: How to get Students to Read Feedback," *Cult of Pedagogy*, 2017, cultofpedagogy.com/delayed-grade

7. Discipline

In an effort to gather more meaningful and effective data, our school behavior team created an office discipline referral (ODR) that would help us to track exactly what was happening and would better align with our school-wide behavior plan. Big data was a big deal at the time, and we thought we could systematically use the data from the ODRs to make better decisions about supporting teachers and students with behavior needs. We had a lot of externalizing behaviors and thought this would be a good idea.

With the new school-wide behavior plan and referral form, we quickly saw a drop in ODRs across our school. We took some time to celebrate and reflect on why our ODRs decreased. We quickly learned that teachers were still having the behavior issues (although not quite as many) but the forms were too much to fill out. We had spent a lot of time designing this form and, until it was out in the wild, we had thought that it was a good form that teachers would be fine with filling out. We were wrong.

Are your behavior forms too much for the teachers to fill out? Since then, I've consulted with many schools on the restructuring of discipline processes, and many don't determine if the forms they are creating are actually worth the time it takes to complete them.

8. Response to intervention

If our goal is to truly educate every child, how difficult is it for teachers to get additional support for students in their classroom? Do you have a solid solution for each level of need for your students? Is this easy to access for teachers and students alike?

9. Special education referrals

It is not typical for students to develop a disability over time. It's a matter of whether or not the educators and parents recognize the needs of the student and react. Sometimes, a student's disability is not identified through testing because the process for gaining access to testing is too difficult for a teacher to navigate. If you are an elementary leader, this is especially important. Your district has a flowchart somewhere that lists the process, and that needs to be followed. What you can do, however, is to identify other ways that you can simplify and ease the burden on teachers for special education referrals. Documenting interventions and their results is certainly an area that you can work to improve for teachers.

10. Other special-education-specific issues

Many educators like to say something like, "It's special education and that is federal law, so there is no flexibility." This is not entirely true. Many of the things we set up for special education vary from district to district and from school to school. For example, the requirement in the Individuals with Disabilities Education Act states that one general education teacher must attend an individualized education program meeting.

The rule at my school is: if the child's disability does *not* impact your class, you do not have to attend the IEP meeting; otherwise you should be there. Yes, this requires an extra meeting that five in seven teachers usually don't attend, but it is much easier for teachers to give kids what they need, when they need it, if the teachers all understand a student's disability and the plan the school has in place to address it. It is important to know the aspects of special education that are unalterable and adapt everything else to your school's specific needs and abilities.

11. State testing

Examine how much effort is required of teachers when it comes to state testing. Although I believe it is unethical for teachers to administer tests that have an impact on their profession, we are still in a position where teachers often have to administer these assessments. As leaders, we must minimize this burden as much as possible. As many standardized tests have moved to a digital assessment, the tasks associated with paper copies of tests have diminished, but we still have work to do in this area. Think about your mandatory testing structure and what you can do to make it less of a burden for teachers.

12. Material checkout

How difficult is it for your teachers to check out a classroom, cart, or lab? How difficult is it to check out books and other materials? One principal told me, "We are in the paper business. There should never be a shortage of paper in our school." When teachers don't have to hoard materials, but know they can get the materials they need, when they need them, they are much more productive and effective.

13. Character education

We can't teach character in a silo. Character is built through experiences and "teachable moments." Yet many of us use one-off lessons to teach students to be the kind of people we want them to be.

Character education must be incorporated into every lesson, every day, to have the necessary impact on kids. Parents can't do it alone and neither can we. We must all work together to make it happen. Can you remove some of these one-off lessons for teachers and help them to incorporate character education into their everyday teaching?

Reflect

Did your action in the prototype stage actually make things easier or less burdensome for your teachers? Here are some questions you can ask yourself.

- Did teachers cheer when you lifted the request placed on them? If you identify something that everyone believes is a waste of time, teachers will cheer when you remove that burden.
- How many of your teachers have expressed relief about the changes you have made?
- What things are not getting done that were getting done before? Is there something that you took away that is actually not missed by anyone?

Iterate

Repeat this process until your expectations on your teachers are as minimal as they can be, while still aligned to your vision for what education should look like in your school. You and I both know that teachers will heap tremendous expectations on themselves, so be sure to reassess those expectations with regularity.

Teachers work hard. There is no doubt about that. We need them to work smarter and we, as leaders, need to not be barriers to teachers. We don't take things off their plate so their job is easier. We take things off their plate so they are able to expend their energy on the thing that matters most: educating kids.

What next?

I had a conversation with a grade-level of teachers one time. We had been working through many of the things we've discussed here. I had removed barriers for them, made a bunch of improvements, and done everything we could think of. The job is never over, so these teachers still had a list of things they needed to be fixed. But there was a difference now. Instead of these teachers complaining about their situation and what they saw as inequities, they were eager to work with me on solutions.

You're probably never going to fix all the issues that exist, but there's a very good chance that you can find solutions collaboratively.

PART 3
The student experience

I have a rule in my school that I never let a student go into a classroom upset. No matter what has happened, they know that I will always listen, and save them from the discomfort that comes with walking into a room with tears streaming down your face.

One time, I was walking in the hall and came across a student crying as she was heading to class. This student is usually always laughing. I talked to her and found out that she had just gotten in trouble with a substitute teacher. The sub had basically said that the student was in trouble with her, and would be in trouble with the regular teacher when he got back, because the sub was right and the student was wrong. Because the sub was an adult and she was a child.

In these situations, kids think the whole world is against them, especially if they are between the ages of five and 18! As I invited the student to sit in my comfy principal chair, she said, "It doesn't matter what happened, because everyone is going to listen to the adult and not to me, because I'm just a kid."

I said, "Try me. I'll listen."

After pausing for a few seconds, she decided to take me up on my offer. She told me her story and I listened. She admitted where she was wrong and I was able to recognize her restraint for not yelling back at the sub, even though she felt very wronged by the situation.

We finished our discussion and I told her a lame dad-joke to get her to smile again. She laughed and was ready to head back to class.

I tell this story as a reminder that listening to students takes very little time but can make a huge difference to them. That student is "enrolled," as the entrepreneur Seth Godin puts it,[19] because she knows that someone will listen to her.

In part 3, we are going to talk about the student experience. First we will look at the environment: what the students feel by attending your school. Some might say this is touchy-feely, mushy stuff, but it is really quite vital. In the three schools where I have been an administrator, I have taken very specific actions to create an environment that empowers students. I always treat them like the young adults they are, which means that I treat them with respect. I believe that they have the power within them to become greater than any of us can imagine. Because of my faith, I see each one as a valuable, powerful son or daughter of God, and that means a lot to me. It also constantly reminds me of their potential for greatness.

I recognize that I cannot force any student to do anything, and sometimes this approach breeds frustration among teachers. I know that I must use my power to suspend with great discretion. And I understand the immense influence I have over students, which will affect their lives for years to come.

We have all that teacher that we will never forget. Sometimes we remember them for good things, sometimes for bad things. Likewise, kids are going to remember us. So, let's make it for something good.

Learner profiles

A great tool to help you create the right environment for your students is a learner profile assessment. Kelly Tenkely, the principal of Anastasis Academy in Denver, Colorado, says, "When you know students as well as we do, you see very quickly that the 'curriculum' is not a match for your students." So, in Tenkely's school, the students are given a learner profile assessment that helps the teachers to know them better. Using three card sets designed through Tenkely's Learning Genome Project,[20] the teachers

---

19 Seth Godin, "Education is Not the Same Thing as Learning," *Medium*, 2019, tinyurl.com/y3roz6s7
20 thelearninggenomeproject.com

hold hour-long conversations with kids. As with most frameworks, the value isn't in labeling students, but rather in the conversations that the framework allows you to have.

The first card set is based on Howard Gardner's theory of eight distinct intelligences. This may be a controversial subject in our current educational climate, but there is still benefit in discussing these intelligences. Using a Likert scale, students rate themselves on statements such as: I am in charge, I daydream, I like to dance, I'm concerned about the environment, and I like to think. As the students rate themselves, you start to see their strengths in each intelligence area. But it is also vital to have conversations about *why* they rate themselves as they do. Saying things like, "I noticed you were a five really fast on that one, tell me more about that" will help them to articulate the reasons for their choices.

The second card set relates to learning styles. Students respond "like me," "sometimes like me," or "not like me" to statements including: I like to doodle, I am easily distracted, I fidget, and I repeat things to myself. Although we understand that kids can learn in any learning style, gaining an understanding of where they are most comfortable and what they want to do will help tremendously as teachers plan learning activities, assessments, and classroom spaces. Imagine knowing at the outset of the year what your students' preferred learning styles are!

The third card set relates to brain dominance. We know that everybody uses both sides of their brain, but these cards help teachers to better understand their students' personalities and learning preferences. Students respond "like me" or "not like me" to statements such as: I'm flexible, I like to work alone, I like bright lights, I like working outside, and I like to build things.

The information collected at Tenkely's school does not define the student, but it does provide insight into their preferences, learning styles, and desires. It is organized in a profile document that allows teachers to learn a lot about the student at a glance. The document also includes answers to a series of questions about the student's interests and passions (books, movies, people, things that make me happy, etc.). The teachers have access to a wealth of knowledge that will help them to design the most beneficial learning experiences for each young person.

I was not a great student, especially in high school. My ninth-grade Honors English teacher would roll over in her grave if she knew that I have become an English teacher myself, and that I am also a principal, writing a book for educators! She kicked me out of all Honors classes in that school because she didn't like my behavior. She didn't try to reach me, she just made decisions that are still affecting me today. Because of what she did, I couldn't take any AP classes, which is what I was on track to do. She told me that the sanctity of her classroom was more important than me and my future. I don't hold a grudge against her (any more) and I've been able to be successful in spite of the impact she had, but it took a few years and a lot of unnecessary pain.

We must remember that we can impact the lives of our students in a powerful way. Imagine if this teacher had completed a learner profile assessment with me. What could that have done to help me be successful in her classroom? And, more importantly, what could that have done to *help the teacher* to help me be successful in her classroom?

Success skills for every student

In his book *The Formative Five*,[21] Thomas Hoerr suggests that there are five success skills that we should focus on just as much as the three Rs. They are grit, empathy, embracing diversity, self-control, and integrity. Hoerr states that these are important, but I'm going to take it a step further and say that if we don't teach these five success skills, then we haven't done our job as educators. We can all learn how to read, write, and do math. Where kids truly need help is in fighting the natural tendencies of man to shirk these success skills.

Sadly, our educational system is built on compliance and adherence to authority. "Because I said so" is a refrain heard much too often in our schools. In the story I shared about the student I found crying in the hall, that student believed, and for good reason, that the adults in her schools did not really care about her as an individual and were not going to listen to her. What she needed to know was that she was worthy of respect no matter whom she was interacting with.

---

21 Thomas R. Hoerr, *The Formative Five: fostering grit, empathy, and other success skills every student needs*, ASCD, 2016

This can be a challenging approach for teachers. Not because teachers are bad, or because they intentionally hurt kids, but because they grew up in a system focused on authoritarian leadership. They thrived in that system, and they went to college and continued in that system. But we are all accountable if we are not doing things that support kids to grow up to be thinking individuals. It used to be that education was the key to a successful life. And although education is still important, the world is changing. Anybody can learn anything, without attending a school. Schools need to shine in creating an environment where students are given freedom of thought and speech. Too many of our schools do not have this.

In part 1, I talked about Chris Wejr, who is an elementary school principal in British Columbia, Canada. When I spoke to him for my podcast, Wejr made a huge impact on my thinking as it relates to student discipline and adult interactions with students. Wejr wants all young people to develop grit, empathy, and integrity – from the young kindergartners all the way up to the high-schoolers. At times, this is easier said than done.

Wejr says that the best way you can help students to overcome their struggles and negative behavior is by making sure they feel a connection to the school. When kids are connected, or "enrolled", they are more likely to think about the impact of their choices.

At Tenkely's school, the information gleaned from the learner profile session is not only valuable to the teacher, but also to the student. It is very important that students understand who they are in order for them to reach their full potential. This is not lip service, but a major part of giving kids the skills they need for success.

As I say throughout this book, there is no one right answer. There are multiple ways to do things, but having a framework of some sort really helps the conversation to go from one of critique to one of growth. Tenkely, Hoerr, and Wejr all provide ample ways to help students gain the success skills they need.

Special education

You can support kids to make better choices by having an inclusive school. Hoerr includes embracing diversity as one of his success skills.

This means that we need to welcome and embrace not only students of all races and ethnicities, but also students with disabilities.

Keven Barker, principal of Ridgeline Academy in Phoenix, Arizona, is at the forefront of this practice in his school. All his special education students are embraced in the general education setting, with support. Barker says this is vital to ensure that those kids are able to live up to their potential. He states simply, "If we never expose them to grade-level material, how can we ever expect them to learn grade-level material?"

Some people believe that "special" kids should be kept away from others. That gifted kids should have their own classes and kids with disabilities should have their own classes, too. I believe that if we want to create an environment that truly embraces diversity, we must not only welcome those students, but also go out of our way to ensure that they are able to get the most out of their education.

Barker shares a fascinating story. A parent complained to him about a girl with Down syndrome being in her son's third-grade class, claiming that the student was bringing down the level of math instruction for everyone because she couldn't possibly be as capable as the others. The general ed class should only have kids in it that are on grade level, the parent asserted.

Barker responded, "Yes, ma'am, we are concerned about students who are below grade level who hold the rest of the kids back. She's actually not the lowest student in the class. I'd like to talk about how to help the kids that are lower than her. There's one student in particular that you and I should talk about, as he is considerably lower than her: your son. How can we help him?"

To Barker, all kids really means all kids. When adults model the embracing and accepting of diversity, students are more likely to do the same.

Start with strengths

One of the best ways to embrace everyone's diversity is to start with their strengths. It is fairly easy to identify strengths in most kids, when you look beyond academics. One teacher commented about my son that he was a daily positive contributor to the classroom environment. That's a good comment. This teacher saw more than academics in my son's ability.

She saw that he was contributing to something bigger than himself and making sure that others were valued in the classroom as well.

Dr. Kimberly Miles, principal of East Gresham Elementary School in Oregon, calls these kinds of notes "soft data" (we've got to come up with a better word than soft when talking about things that are as important as this!). When Miles refers to soft data, she is talking about getting to know the whole child. She asks her teachers to truly understand their students, so that they can make a determination about their soft skills and not only focus on academics.

One of my strengths in high school was that I was the class clown (which I know most teachers would *not* say is a strength). My high school English teacher could have had me in the palm of her hand by simply giving me time to be the clown. Instead, she wanted me to be who she thought was a good student, and I couldn't live up to that.

If she could have found a way to support me in my class-clown tendencies, she would have built trust with me and we could have had a conversation about when the right time is for certain behaviors. You see, I just wanted people to either love me or hate me. I didn't know how to deal with anything in between. Many students are still like that today.

We need to ask kids questions and try to figure out what makes them tick. I worked with a student once who loved everything related to basketball. That was a strength that was easy to pick out. Because he loved everything basketball, he didn't care much for school. As you can imagine, this caused some pretty negative behaviors. And he would really ramp up those negative behaviors during basketball season. You would think that he would behave better when he could play basketball every day after school. Not this guy. It just reminded him that he didn't want to do anything else.

In an effort to understand him better, I sat next to him during a girls' basketball game. Of course, he was trying his best to be Dick Vitale, commenting on every single play and move. This student, who wouldn't talk about anything on-topic in class, was completely engrossed in the game.

So, when he made a comment like, "That player should have passed the ball," I asked him why. And I asked him why again. And again, and again, and again. He loved being able to talk about something he was passionate

113

about. I leaned into his strengths and found out what made him tick. Over the following days, before he could get in trouble and be sent to the office, I would find him and ask him questions about "something I've been thinking about." Most of the time, these conversations were about basketball, but sometimes they weren't. It was amazing to hear what he had to say about a myriad of topics.

Our conversations finally turned to education, and he told me why he was disengaged. He had been watching videos and TED talks about how education can be changed from what it has been in our country for decades. He was disengaged not because he was dumb, but because he knew that the school system wasn't serving him. And he was right. His teachers were all focused on compliance and not learning. For him, that was demoralizing. Once we figured that out (after a couple of weeks), we were able to give him a little more leeway and he had much more success.

It isn't always easy to find students' strengths, but it is certainly worth the effort. Here are three ways to start.

1. Ask the student about what they're interested in.
2. Let the student teach someone about the thing they're interested in.
3. Let the teaching count for something in their life.

Choice and voice

Later, I'll talk more about choice and voice as they relate to learning, but for now we're focusing on the environment that kids experience. Can kids make decisions that are impactful for the entire school? What I mean is: is that even possible?

Let's look at a couple of examples. First, dress code. Does it really matter what a student wears to school? In some cases, yes. But, for the most part, a student's clothing doesn't really make much difference day-to-day. And yet it seems that we are always focused on that single document that contains so many provisions and restrictions and different ideas that there is no way to make any sense of it, other than to see it as an act of control.

And honestly, most of our school day is about control and compliance. We don't teach kids to learn so much as we teach them to be obedient to an authority figure. The bell rings and kids are supposed to move. The bell rings again and kids are marked tardy, lectured, or locked out of class if they are late. Let's think about that for a moment: why do we prevent kids from entering the learning environment if they are late? We basically say, "OK, kids, you are late, so even if you were trying to be here, you are not allowed to come in." That makes no sense!

Another example is suspensions. The punishment of a suspension is often completely unwarranted. When we suspend a student, we give away all power that we could have possibly had over that student. One of my favorite items of ridiculousness is the idea of suspending kids as a consequence for being truant. It's hilarious! We tell the student who is *deliberately* missing school that they are not allowed to come to school. What are we thinking? But that goes for nearly all suspendable behaviors. In most situations, there really isn't much sense in suspending kids. Where suspension does make sense for me is when violence is involved. It is a very clear way of saying that we don't want this behavior in our school and we can't allow it.

Many schools use positive behavior interventions and supports, which usually means, "We give kids rewards for good behavior, because it's better than only punishing the bad kids and spending all our time on them." One key tenet of this approach is that teachers will give each student four positive recognitions for every one negative recognition. I've got to tell you, focusing on positive behavior is a step in the right direction. But it often goes overboard.

Chris Wejr has a great story that illustrates how this can backfire. An elementary school student helped to take another kid who had been hurt down to the office. She was being kind, considerate, and a good friend. When she delivered the student to Mr. Wejr, he thanked her and recognized her for the kindness she had displayed. She hung around for a minute and then impatiently asked, "Where is my Eagle Buck?" You see, in that school, they gave kids Eagle Bucks as rewards for good deeds. This girl seemed to be a good friend, but when she demanded her Eagle Buck, she betrayed a darker secret: she was in it for the money!

That moment changed Wejr's perspective. He doesn't want kids to help someone because they will be rewarded, but because it is the right thing to do. He also wants to show true gratitude to kids who are doing the right things. It's very hard and it takes a dedicated educator to balance those two seemingly competing values. Sometimes we will mess up – and that is OK.

Reaching out to the students who struggle

This is perhaps the most important thing we can do. As I've mentioned before, we have an amazing opportunity for growth with kids who are really struggling. Paul Erickson, an elementary principal in Kansas, wisely told me, "That's the only student you'll be called back to the building for, so why not [take some extra time with them]." He was talking about the need to work with and pay special attention to those kids who always seem to be getting into trouble.

Dr. Amy Fast, principal at McMinnville High School in Oregon, surveyed every single student to see what their school environment was like. She asked them to help her understand if what they were doing as a school was worthwhile. Fast felt that her schools' student surveys were too lame to be answered by her students – they were seeking feedback, but they weren't extracting any useful data. The surveys were essentially a waste of time for staff and students alike.

"Our staff didn't know students as individuals," Fast told me. So the team created a way to get to know them as individuals. They gave them a blunt, non-anonymous survey, and Fast and the other admin team members went to each class to speak to the students before they took the survey.

Fast prepped the kids for questions like the ones below:

- Are you hopeful?
- Do your teachers care?
- Do you have a connection to one staff member?
- Do you have friends?
- Do you feel like you matter?
- Have you ever experienced discrimination?
- Would you report something bad that happened?

Once the students had completed the survey, the team coded the data and determined who was not connected to the school. In this large comprehensive high school, they made a list of the 100 most disconnected kids and found a way to individually connect to each one. Then they found ways to help the students whose answers indicated that they needed help.

It isn't enough to simply *get* the data, Fast says. People need to make changes in response to the data. The results of her survey led to changes in professional development for the teachers at McMinnville High School, and one thing that Fast and her team saw was that exit slips with students were more personal and meaningful in nature.

Although this ongoing project takes considerable time regularly, it also solidifies the need in the minds of staff to make things better for each individual student. When I asked her about making so many significant changes, Fast's response was simple: "What's best for students is also best for teachers!"

We can use our design-thinking process to do a similar thing:

- **Empathy.** Take a look through your policies and practices for student behavior and see what kind of an environment your policies create. Ask your students how connected they feel to the school. Be prepared for dishonest answers – there is a good chance that they don't trust you.
- **Prototype.** Find one way you can start changing things by yourself. It can be as simple as committing to listen to every student's story, if you aren't already.
- **Reflect.** Do kids feel more connected? Can you see in their eyes and by how they act that they care more than they seemed to before?
- **Iterate.** Keep making changes to make your school environment more student-friendly.

The importance of trust

What does it look like to trust students? With so many scary things happening in our world, school safety has overcome our ability to trust students. Look at the policy manual for any school district and you will see that the policies contained therein are really designed to deal with the fewer than 5% of students who do something wrong. The reality is that we make draconian rules when the vast majority of students are doing what they should be doing, nearly all the time. This gives credence to the idea that schools are akin to prisons, and to the idea of a school-to-prison pipeline.

What are some simple ways that you can start showing your students that you trust them? Let's look at hall passes first.

When students need to use hall passes, we are telling them that they need to be able to account for where they are in the school, right? That seems pretty benign. What happens if you actually trust that students are where they are supposed to be? You see, you need a different perspective when you start with trust. A hall pass is a little thing to us adults, but a very big thing to students, because ditching the hall pass can have huge implications for the student experience.

And what about bathroom breaks? Do *you* ask permission to use the bathroom when you are in a learning environment, or do you have enough respect for yourself to take care of business when you need to? Whenever I teach a class, I tell students that they don't need to ask to use the restroom. In fact, I tell them that I don't even want to know they need to use it. I just want them to get up, leave, use the restroom, and come back. If they abuse that, then we have to talk about it, and I'd much rather talk about what we are learning than talk about the bathroom. The response from kids never ceases to surprise me. They act like I have just given them the keys to the kingdom! They are always overjoyed that I trust them enough to do this.

You see, this really goes back to the idea of compliance being the main driver in our schools. We have to focus on *learning* as the main driver. What is the experience for students in our schools? It's about rules that are designed to keep out the worst behaviors, even if that means students are forced into an awful situation.

We all want to be safe when flying and we let safety become the driver in airports, allowing the great invasions of privacy that happen in airports all across the country. We fall into the same trap at schools. Many schools state that "safety is our number one priority!" Although I appreciate that sentiment and I want to ensure that all kids are safe in schools, I do not believe that we have schools for the express purpose of keeping kids safe. We have schools so students can learn.

I'm a big fan of the book *The One Thing*[22] by Gary Keller with Jay Papasan. It starts with the proverb "He who chases two rabbits catches none." When we focus on more than one priority, we accomplish nothing. If our priority in schools is safety, then it is not learning. We can only have one. What priority do we want to have?

The educator and consultant Allison Zmuda asks us to pay attention to four things to show students that we trust them:

1. **Voice** – allowing students to have a voice in the process.
2. **Co-creation** – giving students a seat at the design table.
3. **Social construction** – ensuring that students are interacting with peers.
4. **Self-discovery** – helping kids to look back on what they got better at.

Let's look at each one briefly in terms of how it relates to trust.

Voice

When you allow students to use their own voices, you are trusting them to make good decisions. Zmuda told me that this is important from a school- or system-wide perspective. But I would add that it also has value in the smallest of settings: in individual work with students. When we give kids voice, we tell them they can create something that matters. It is more than just giving them a little choice here and there.

I found that teaching voice to middle-school students was very challenging. It was always so easy to know when a student "got it" and so much harder to explain, "This is what voice is like." But as students became more aware of what their own voice was, they sought to use it more frequently.

One great example is when a student got to write a poem and his "street talk" was actually appropriate. Well, I called it a poem – he called it rap. He couldn't believe that I let him use slang and shortened words, because in our essay writing, he certainly couldn't. I think I got a lesson that day, too.

Co-creation

Most educators would call this choice, but I love the idea that goes along with "creation." If students are involved in creating a learning

---

22 Gary Keller with Jay Papasan, *The One Thing*, John Murray Learning, 2014

environment or a learning activity, we are telling them that they are important.

One teacher related a story to me about how she gave her students a seat at the design table. She asked them what kinds of things they wanted to learn about in science. The students generated a list with her help, and she started brainstorming ideas for lesson plans. Soon, the kids had a plan for what they wanted to learn from her. These sixth-grade students were no longer passively sitting and waiting for the lesson to start – they were eagerly seeking, because they couldn't wait for her to share with them what she had learned.

You could take this one step further and have the students be part of the teaching process as well, but…baby steps.

Social construction

Most students, at any age, crave interaction with their peers. One of my main challenges when I am facilitating a discussion is to keep my mouth shut! I want that interaction as well, but I know that the learning opportunity is not for me. Zmuda encourages us to find ways to help students interact as much as possible. So many times, the conversation is where the powerful learning takes place, and yet we only "count" the written documentation of learning. Students learn by doing, just like adults, and when they are able to engage with their peers, much more learning happens than we can catch on a worksheet.

The challenge with social construction is keeping it relevant and focused. Many educators struggle when it spins out of control and students are no longer socially constructing. Their behavior is more akin to demolition!

In these moments, a reset needs to occur. Students need to be guided back to the norms for behavior in a trusting way. This is where trust lives and, sadly, dies. If we allow the social construction only until "I've had it!", students learn that we are not really serious about it. But if we explain norms and social expectations in our classroom, and engage students to assist with the enforcement, they can see that we trust them to get back on task.

Self-discovery

I love Zmuda's use of "self-discovery" rather than self-reflection. When students have the opportunity to look back on what they improved at, they discover that they are better than they ever thought. And what I love about this is that it also signifies trust. We trust them when we give them time to think about and process what happened, and how it impacted them. Sometimes they discover areas that need growth, and sometimes they see that they are only able to focus on things that they did well.

There's no right or wrong answer. And when we trust them to come to their own conclusions, we show them that there is not always a right answer, and that each answer is unique to each student.

Learning to trust

Now it's time for you to reflect. What does trust look like at your school? Do your school policies invite or erode trust with students? What is one action that you can take to show you trust students?

At my Title 1 school, with 85% attendance, we tried everything to get students to come to school. We were doing great things academically, but we couldn't reach the 15% of students who weren't there. We threw parties, gave incentives, promised big rewards to students with perfect attendance, and none of those things worked. The one thing that made an impact, and continues to make an impact, was trusting the students.

We co-created by asking some students what could get them to 95% average daily attendance. They didn't even know what that meant. Then we asked them to involve their friends. We gave them a seat at the design table and invited social construction. Finally, we let them reflect on what they had learned.

The solution we co-created was that every day we would announce the average attendance for each grade. When a grade reached 95% attendance, those kids could cheer and yell and scream for five seconds. That's it. That was voice. To get the full picture of this, you really have to watch my TEDxCSDTeachers talk entitled "Simplicity."[23] Six-hundred kids screaming is a sight to behold!

---

23 youtu.be/Xz_zKCgCLnQ

121

In just a few short days, attendance skyrocketed to 95%. It stayed there until the end of that year, and continued into the next year, and the next, and the next. As long as the school kept announcing the daily attendance, the students were at 95% or better. It doesn't always take a lot to inspire kids – sometimes it's as simple as a quick cheer.

Making connections

When you see a student in the hall, ask them a question. When you are working with students, ask them questions. You'll catch more bees with honey, and a sincere "What are you working on?" will build a relationship while you figure out what is going on with that student.

I recently visited some pretty amazing schools and saw this in effect. At Design39Campus in Poway, just outside of San Diego, California, I saw kids working in the hall. I saw students moving from one place to another regularly. It almost seemed like the kids didn't really have classrooms. They just had working spaces all throughout the school. Instead of teachers being annoyed by kids' roaming tendencies, I saw many teachers asking questions:

- What are you working on?
- Where are you heading?
- What do you need help with?
- Who is supporting you?

The students didn't need hall passes or anything else, because they were focused and determined to do what was right. It was spectacular.

Kelly Tenkely says that we are giving kids "apprenticeships in the art of learning." That's a different perspective than filling their heads full of knowledge, and it really gets at the core of what we should be doing with students every day. We should be teaching them how to learn, unlearn, and relearn, so that when they are adults, they can be ready for whatever the world throws at them.

Growth mindset

Are you allowed to write a book about education without a section on growth mindset? This topic may have even been beaten to death, so I will take a slightly different approach. As it relates to the design-thinking process, growth mindset has a pretty narrow focus. It's about believing that your product can be made better with feedback. I'm going to let other authors tell the story of why mindset matters and what people can do about it. I invite you to read Carol Dweck's book *Mindset: the new psychology of success.*[24]

One of the ways to apply what Dweck teaches in *Mindset* is to speak aspirationally to students. The educator Sylwia Denko does this well. When her students make a mistake, her response is always, "It's OK, it helps your brain to grow." You see, she takes the time at the beginning of the year to teach her students that when they make mistakes, it actually helps their brains to form new neural connections. This is truly a powerful experience for her students.

Throughout the year, Denko teaches 10 lessons that she designed to show students what a growth mindset looks like. But kids still make mistakes. In her book *The Gift of Failure*,[25] the teacher and writer Jessica Lahey shares a story that really hits the nail on the head. She had her back to the class when she felt something whizz by her head. It was a mechanical pencil. She pulled the culprit aside and asked what he had been thinking just before he threw the pencil.

Lahey writes: "He looked at his feet and shuffled them around a bit. 'Nothing.' He looked up at me and shrugged again. 'I didn't know I was going to throw the pencil until I'd thrown it, and by then, it was too late.'"

Sometimes kids don't really understand what they are doing. Sometimes they don't appear to have a growth mindset because they don't appear to have a mind at all! If we want kids to learn from their mistakes, we must *ask them* what they can learn from their mistakes. According to Lahey, "The key to helping kids curb their impulsive behavior is to teach them how to understand their patterns of conduct and the body language that tends to precede these behaviors." When they can see that they actually

---

24 Carol S. Dweck, *Mindset: the new psychology of success*, Random House, 2006
25 Jessica Lahey, *The Gift of Failure*, Harper Collins, 2016

have control over their bodies and their minds, they will be able to grow and learn in a much more powerful way.

Part of our problem in education is that we have set up a system where students pass or fail. Succeed or fail. Get it or are stupid. We have set up too many dichotomies, when in reality we have gradients of excellence or failure. There is so much gray area. So, in my view, having a growth mindset is more about teaching students how they can continue to learn past a due date, and figuring out how to make their learning more relevant and meaningful to them.

We need to recognize that learning doesn't happen in little chunks. Learning happens anywhere and everywhere, and turning in an assignment doesn't mean that the learning stops. Learning can and should continue beyond that.

Responsive vs proactive classrooms

Let's talk about responsive classrooms. According to the organization Responsive Classroom, this is "a student-centered, social and emotional learning approach to teaching and discipline. It is comprised of a set of research, and evidence-based practices designed to create safe, joyful, and engaging classrooms and school communities for both students and teachers."

The Responsive Classroom website[26] set outs the four key domains of a responsive classroom:

1. **Engaging academics**. Teachers create learning tasks that are active, interactive, appropriately challenging, purposeful, and connected to students' interests.
2. **Positive community**. Teachers nurture a sense of belonging, significance, and emotional safety so that students feel comfortable taking risks and working with a variety of peers.
3. **Effective management**. Teachers create a calm, orderly environment that encourages autonomy and allows students to focus on learning.
4. **Developmentally responsive teaching**. Teachers use knowledge of

---

26 responsiveclassroom.org

child development, along with observations of students, to create a developmentally appropriate learning environment.

I believe that responsive classrooms is a powerful practice, but the inclusion of the word "responsive" concerns me. The dictionary definition of responsive is "reacting quickly or positively."[27] But rather than responding or reacting to the kids in front of us, I think we need to make an effort to create *proactive* classrooms.

The dictionary definition of proactive is "creating or controlling a situation by causing something to happen rather than responding to it after it has happened."[28] Let me attempt to summarize my proactive classroom approach:

A proactive classroom sets students up for success by preparing for, planning for, and adapting learning opportunities to students' diverse needs and interests, and by knowing the students well enough to make decisions ahead of time that will meet their needs.

There are four main components:

1. **Adult belief system**. Teachers believe that students are capable of accomplishing tasks that can change the world.
2. **Relevance**. Each learning opportunity is infused with meaning that is relevant to the student. If a learning opportunity does not relate to the student's life, it should not be used. The link to learning and a student's current or future success is imperative to every learning opportunity.
3. **Facilitation**. Rather than being directors of learning, teachers are facilitators of learning who guide students to where they need to be and what they need to learn. Teachers have a broad understanding of standards of learning for students and can identify ways that students can learn meaningfully and proactively.
4. **Soft skills** (there's that word "soft" again!). Student soft skills are not a secondary goal or an add-on. Collaboration, growth mindset,

---

27 lexico.com/en/definition/responsive
28 lexico.com/en/definition/proactive

resilience, grit, communication, overcoming anger and frustration, and many others are useful skills that are prepared for and emphasized on a regular basis.

As you will see below, there are *a lot* of soft skills, so it's impossible to focus on each of these individually. What we need to do is find a way to teach these constantly. If we are a proactive classroom, I believe we will have a much better chance of accomplishing that. Imagine for a moment if these skills were the only thing you taught in your school. How would your instructional model change?

And what would parents say about your school if these skills were measured more than math and other subject areas? I think they would be very happy.

But here's the problem: we can't just teach these in isolation. They have to be part of a bigger plan. They have to be addressed repeatedly and over time. They need to be revisited often and made prominent in all that we do. I truly believe that if these skills were the only things we taught in school, we would create great adults.

As part of an assessment he created to help adults (and kids) determine their own level of soft skills, my good friend Tom Bay identified the following soft skills. Review the list below and circle the three that you think are the most critical for student success. It's very difficult. Maybe try circling the three categories that you believe are the most important. It's hard to decide if self-control is more important than perception, but it is a worthwhile endeavor to try to choose just a few.

Soft skill	Category	Soft skill	Category
Ability to deliver clear and useful criticism	Influence	Authenticity and consistent behavior	Self-control
Adaptability to changing requirements	Self-control	Body language (reading and delivering)	Influence
Agility in the face of unexpected obstacles	Self-control	Bouncing back from failure	Self-control
Alacrity and the ability to start and stop quickly	Self-control	Charisma and the skill to influence others	Influence
		Clarity in language and vision	Influence
Artistic sense and good taste	Wisdom	Coachability and the desire to coach others	Self-control
Assertiveness on behalf of ideas that matter	Influence	Collaborative mindset	Self-control
Attention to detail	Productivity	Compassion for those in need	Self-control

Soft skill	Category	Soft skill	Category
Competitiveness	Self-control	Listening skills	Productivity
Conflict-resolution instincts	Wisdom	Living in balance	Self-control
Conscientiousness in keeping promises	Self-control	Managing difficult conversations	Self-control
Creativity in the face of challenges	Wisdom	Managing up	Productivity
		Map-making	Perception
Crisis-management skills	Productivity	Meeting hygiene	Productivity
Critical thinking instead of mere compliance	Wisdom	Mentoring	Wisdom
Customer-service passion	Self-control	Motivated to take on new challenges	Self-control
Dealing with difficult people	Wisdom	Negotiation skills	Influence
Decision-making with effectiveness	Productivity	Networking	Influence
		Passionate	Self-control
Delegation for productivity	Productivity	Persuasive	Influence
Design thinking	Perception	Planning for projects	Productivity
Diplomacy in difficult situations	Wisdom	Posture for forward motion	Self-control
		Presentation skills	Influence
Dispute-resolution skills	Influence	Problem solving	Productivity
Eagerness to learn from criticism	Self-control	Public speaking	Influence
Emotional intelligence	Self-control	Purpose	Self-control
Empathy for customers, co-workers, and vendors	Wisdom	Quick-wittedness	Self-control
		Reframing	Influence
Endurance for the long haul	Self-control	Research skills	Productivity
Enthusiasm for the work	Self-control	Resilience	Self-control
Entrepreneurial thinking and guts	Productivity	Risk-taking	Self-control
		Self-awareness	Self-control
Ethics even when not under scrutiny	Self-control	Self-confidence	Self-control
		Selling skills	Influence
Etiquette	Self-control	Sense of humor	Self-control
Facilitation of discussion	Productivity	Social skills	Wisdom
Fashion instinct	Perception	Storytelling	Influence
Flexibility	Self-control	Strategic thinking	Perception
Friendliness	Self-control	Strategic thinking taking priority over short-term gamesmanship	Self-control
Giving feedback without ego	Influence		
Goal-setting skills	Productivity		
Honesty	Self-control	Stress management	Self-control
Influence	Influence	Supervising with confidence	Wisdom
Innovative problem-solving techniques	Productivity	Talent management	Influence
		Team-building	Influence
Inspiring to others	Influence	Technology savvy	Productivity
Intercultural competence	Wisdom	Time management	Productivity
Interpersonal skills	Influence	Tolerance of change and uncertainty	Self-control
Judging people and situations	Perception		
Lateral thinking	Productivity	Troubleshooting	Productivity
Leadership	Influence	Writing for impact	Influence
Lean techniques	Productivity		

The learning experience

So, now that we have talked about the student experience as it relates to their environment, I want to look at the learning experience we set up for our students. Much of what I say will also be applicable to how teachers learn. It's funny how sometimes we bring in professional development leaders and they spend the whole time lecturing our staff on how they shouldn't lecture to their students. We need to move past that.

We need to ask the question: what's it for? What is school for and how can we make it more meaningful for our students?

Over the next few pages, we will use my proactive classroom approach to explore some ways that we can create and control a situation that causes students to be engaged in their learning. As we talk about the student learning experience, we must be aware of the impact that this also has on teachers and parents. Many of the ideas I suggest are not new, but still fundamentally change how a school is run. Change, as you know, is hard. But it's less hard for our students and they can adapt to it very easily.

Setting goals

In my family, we set goals. Every Sunday night, we have a family council; we talk about things that are going on and we set goals. Last year, my then-kindergartner set a goal to be a reader by the end of the year. She wanted to read chapter books. Her weekly goals quickly became about reading, and she devoted lots of time and effort to the task. Guess what happened? She learned to read. By June, she was reading chapter books. It was very exciting – not that she was practicing her letters all the time, but that she had set a goal and worked hard to achieve it.

When kids have a challenge in front of them and the ability to persevere to make it a reality, it is an amazing thing to behold.

It can be really effective to have students work on a project for an entire year. When we create projects for students to work on, we should think again about Allison Zmuda's four things that show students we trust them.

1. **Voice.** For my daughter, this meant that she was able to set her own goal.
2. **Co-creation.** In my family, our kids set their goals and we do very little to influence them, until they set a goal that is too weak for their ability. When it is too weak for them, we push them to create something more applicable to their skill level.
3. **Social construction.** So little of what we do today is done in a silo. We are frequently interacting with others and kids really benefit from this.
4. **Self-discovery.** I remember very distinctly helping my daughter to look back on her process of learning to read. She, I hope, learned that her hard work and determination were what made her successful.

If we look at these four elements, we can easily judge whether the project we have co-created with the student is beneficial.

Project-based learning

Students who are engaged in project-based learning learn the "just in time" information they need. Seth Godin is an ardent proponent of this just-in-time way of learning. He says that when the student needs to learn something in order to accomplish something that she is passionate about, she will learn it faster and with greater ease than if she had learned it in a traditional teaching environment. I've certainly seen this to be the case.

Amy Baeder is an educator and an expert on project-based learning. When she talked to me about PBL, she described it in this manner:

"There are a few schools of thought on this. The first is that it's completely free inquiry. That's the definition that scares educators the most. The students make every decision and they can investigate whatever they want.

On the other end of the spectrum is where all of the decisions are made for the kids already. There is no choice. There are certain activities and a test at the end.

Somewhere in the middle is the sweet spot. Where you as a teacher understand what outcome you want for students. It's still very rigorous. You want to ensure every student achieves their goal.

The difference is, it's relevant, it's meaningful, it's engaging, and ideally it's context-specific. For instance, when a project is done in Fairbanks, Alaska, it's obvious it was done in that community. On the other hand, if it's done in Arkansas, the students get the same learning objectives and goals, but it's evident it was done in Arkansas. It's specific to the particular environment and that specific group of kids."

Students in a project-based learning environment learn more skills and reach more standards than kids who receive traditional instruction. When you think about all the different skills that a project requires to be successful, it's no wonder that kids learn so much in this non-traditional format.

My ideal scenario for project-based learning is year-long (or longer) projects that are sparked by an essential question and solve a real problem. Why can't a kindergartner start to solve a problem and continue developing a solution to that problem as they grow and mature? For some reason, we think that we need to isolate learning into chunks that are arbitrary and focus on made-up problems that nobody cares about.

A better option is one project for the whole year, collaboratively worked on with teachers from different content areas. Kids have too many irons in the fire. When I have something important in my life, I focus on that one thing as much as possible until it's done and then I move on to something else.

Training students to excel

Let's take a look at a typical student's day in third grade. It's usual for a student to have 90 minutes focused solely on math, then another 90 minutes on reading, with 30 minutes then devoted to writing. There will be a recess in there and they'll have lunch. Somewhere they will have a "special" class: art, PE, library, music. After that, if they are lucky and the teacher is so inclined, they might get some science and maybe social studies.

For a middle school student with a seven-period day, there will be seven different expectations from seven different teachers and rarely any connections between the classes, even though there might be lots of room for overlap.

Most high school students will have 90 minutes per day of four subjects, and then 90 minutes each of four more subjects the next day. Oh, wait, we know social-emotional stuff is important, so we'll wedge that into an advisory period that isn't beneficial at all and could be considered downtime (or wasted time, if we're being harsh).

Students have this incredible amount of stress on them at any given time. Multiple expectations for learning are placed on them, by multiple teachers, with multiple assignments due that don't relate to each other. Rather than having the opportunity to be successful at any one thing, kids are forced, by design, to be a jack of all trades and a master of none. We aren't really training our students to excel – we are training them to be compliant.

Let's reimagine what this could look like with a different setup. Let's keep it simple and say that we are going to work with middle school students, helping them to create a project that they will work on throughout the year.

The teachers get together and decide that the students that year are going to learn about creating a utopia. Each teacher decides what their subject area will need from the group. Since my teachers actually did this, I share their notes overleaf (loose as they may be) to show that this process is not perfect. The end result was amazing and very beneficial, but it was messy to get there – and that is OK!

This process helped us to clarify what is important to our kids and invited collaboration between teachers and students. Students went from having seven irons in the fire to having just one: the Utopia Project. The teachers benefited, too. They got to work together a lot more than they had before. Of course, all this collaboration led to more conflict. But that conflict forced teachers and students to iron out their differences and figure out what was needed to be supportive of each other.

- Utopia name.
- They pick a partner, then we pair two pairs together to make groups of four.
- They could have a homeroom, then rotate around together?
- Move within those groups OR stay in one assigned class for core classes.
- OR do the above in the last two weeks as a group (maybe science/math – prototype focus?) but keep partners for first two weeks and focus on SS/English research/mapping/reading.

1. Bloom's Digital Taxonomy.
2. Present to everyone.
3. Google site/docs.
4. Transportation – prototype – competition.
5. Thinking questions:
   How is your society different from your current society? What did you add to make it better than your current society?

Social studies

Give your "perfect" utopia community a name and research the five themes of geography for your community – many of these fall under multiple disciplines.

Location – Give absolute and relative locations.

Place – describe physical looks, terrain, climate, population. Draw a detailed map and legend.

Region/human environment interaction (think culture) –
  What holidays, celebrations, festivals.
  How do people spend their day/ what do they do – what job, work, free time?
  Houses.
  Food.
  Resources.

Movement – how do people and goods move about (the transportation piece as well)?

Government – what type of government and details of what positions are to be involved. Name at least two laws citizens must follow.

English

Ideas – possibly look at society in films to compare and change to fit their utopia.

Novels – *The Giver, The City of Ember.*

What we actually will do...

- Opinion section (write an eight-sentence paragraph on how and why your utopia community is better than the current society you live in).

- Headline tragedy/celebration.
- Classified: create three advertisements using the topics from other classes.
- History: legend.
- Mythological creature/mascot of your city.
- Create newspaper articles with topics on two of the following: sports, entertainment, political event, weather, politics, local events/entertainment, public safety report.

Science

Food sources – farming/ranching/fishing.

Medical – standards and practices within the medical community.

Fitness – discuss regular daily activities and how they relate to body systems.

Technology – look into possible technological level for the society and how it will be represented in that society.

Population dynamics – how a population size/density will be regulated.

Math

Prototype for transportation (air, water, land) or buildings.

Architecture (surface area, volume, shapes; trapezoids, triangles, cubes).
Velocity.

Art

De Stijl, the post-war utopian ideal.
What is your utopian art aesthetic?
Design and execute an artwork. Present its mathematical, scientific, political, and philosophical ideals in a video or other online presentation.

Technology/computers

Tech-savvy living, smart homes.
Robotics.
Back to the primitive.

Booths?

Last full day: booths with finished projects. Sales pitch from each group leads to parent voting or questions (creativity, safety, design) on iPad. Kid from each group does GooseChase (QR code links with questions?).

Part day#1: clean up rooms. Design utopian clothes.

Part day#2: clothing contest timed event.

Last day: awards day – parents' choice and kids' choice.

Individual projects

My science teacher has a student with diabetes who wants to understand her disease and what it means for her life. She wants all the information she can get and wants to use school time to do that. She said to my science teacher, "Mrs. Forbes, I wish I could just spend all my science time this year learning more about diabetes, but you have all this other stuff you need to teach us."

Mrs. Forbes, not to be outwitted by a legitimately powerful suggestion, said, "Are you sure about that? I bet that we can make that happen! If you want to learn about diabetes, we will fit it into whatever we are doing." Mrs. Forbes worked with the student to make sure there was depth to her learning about diabetes, and supported her to be successful in that. She also invited other teachers to help this student learn more about diabetes through their classes.

I had a similar situation with a student who was way too advanced for my seventh-grade language arts class. She was doing college-level work for fun, so I had her ditch my content and create her own language arts portfolio project for the year, where she read the books she wanted to read and analyzed them. She had checkpoints instead of due dates and came up with something really spectacular for a seventh-grader.

The real challenge is what to do when students aren't ready or able to do this kind of focused work. I don't have the answer! We are working in my school on creating "stepping stones" to help students build up the skills they need to manage themselves on these kinds of individual or small-group projects.

Getting out of the way

As educators, we often feel that we know the right things to do. The reality is that the world is changing and we need to do things a bit differently. Most teachers were educated in a traditional system and it is very hard for us to overcome those ingrained practices.

I once taught at a school where most teachers had respect and concern for others. One year, we filled out a rubric to see if kids qualified for foreign languages in eighth grade. My big problem with the rubric was that it tended to put all the "good" kids in foreign languages and all the "bad" kids in reading. I raised my concerns and although those with whom I spoke seemed to say, "Well, we know more about the situation than you, so stop making waves," they were supportive after I persisted. This led to some quick changes to the rubric. I suggested that we have an application form for the students to fill out, which would help them to decide if foreign languages were right for them. I was glad that these teachers and counselors were willing to work together to come up with a solution that got us out of students' way.

At the top of the application form,[29] it says: "Learning a new language is a difficult, challenging, and fun experience. Foreign language at Fort Herriman Middle School is considered an Honors class. To enroll in a foreign language, you need to understand that it will be a huge commitment. You must complete daily homework assignments and practice constantly. At Fort Herriman, we don't want you to just get a grade, we want you to actually speak your language. This application will help you decide if a foreign language class is right for you."

The form then asks students to indicate whether they agree or disagree with the following statements, on a Likert scale of 1 (strongly agree) to 5 (strongly disagree).

- I work hard as hard as I can in every class.
- I rarely do as little as possible in every class.
- I just care about getting a good grade in my classes.
- I am interested in learning new things even when not in school.
- I want to learn how to speak a different language.
- I can learn things on my own, without a teacher's help.
- I often learn things on my own, without a teacher's help.
- I rarely miss school.

Next, the form asks the students to add up all the numbers they circled and write down the score. It tells them that if they got less than 18, they might do well in a foreign language class. Then the students need to fill out the following section:

---

29 tinyurl.com/yahbefwt

"I _____ (print your name)
request to be enrolled in French or Spanish (circle one) class for eighth
grade. I realize that this will require _____
_____
_____ (list three things that
a foreign language class requires) from me. I am willing to put in the
extra work effort and practice to be successful."

This process gave kids who might not have been recommended by
their teachers a chance to go for foreign languages. And it also gave kids
who realized they didn't want to learn a foreign language, but would
have been recommended, a chance to opt out of that learning experience.
Fundamentally, I don't believe that we should hold kids back from doing
something they want to do. Their desire to do the thing makes them so
much more capable of achieving success.

Standards-based grading

"But what's my grade?" my student asked me. We were working on a
project that was making a real difference to students, but this question
kept coming up. It was May 2008, and Barack Obama and Hillary
Clinton were squaring off in their political boxing ring to clinch the
Democratic Party nomination for that year's presidential election.
Seventh-graders from around the world were collaborating on building
a wiki about the campaign.

We had partnered with schools in New Zealand, France, and all over
the US. Students researched information about each of the candidates,
learned about their backgrounds, and added the pertinent information
to the wiki. It was an incredible project.

But my students, who kept asking what their grade was, were missing
the bigger picture. They were involved in a conversation about one of
the biggest events in history: the first time an African American had a
shot at the presidency. It was fascinating to see them so excited about
politics – something that kids usually aren't excited about. It was also
disheartening that they kept bugging me about grading their work. You
see, they were creating something meaningful that was a resource for
others. It wasn't about grades.

Thankfully, I figured out a solution very quickly. I started assessing them on the standards they were supposed to reach in seventh grade, rather than grading them on the actual page they had added to the wiki. I gave them a checklist of the standards and said that they would not get a grade, but rather a checkmark for being proficient on the standard. This changed everything. Kids started articulating why their actions demonstrated proficiency. I'd never heard students argue so eloquently on behalf of themselves.

One of the standards listed about 20 prefixes that students were supposed to know. One student went through his contributions to the wiki and found where he had corrected other students' misuse of prefixes. He was able to show that he had learned what he needed to.

As time went on, the students learned that they needed to document their work and come to me with evidence of their learning. At first, they were focused on grades. By the end, they were focused on learning. I am always amazed by the ability of kids to rise to our expectations and do incredible things. Instead of "But what's my grade?" they were asking questions like:

- "How do I demonstrate that I know how to edit my and other students' work?"
- "How can I use figurative language to describe the campaign or the candidate's history?"
- "How can I help my fellow students to edit their work to be more clear?"

Brian Edmister, elementary principal of Genesee Valley Central School in New York, is using standards-based grading in a powerful way. He created a STEAM room and asked each of his teachers to use it at least once over the year. Of course, some teachers only used it one time, while others are happy to spend a lot of time in there.

Students and teachers go into the STEAM room and do some type of learning. When a student accomplishes a standard, they can show that to any adult and "get credit" for that learning. This approach allows students to be constantly learning. As teachers see the great work that kids are doing, they can recognize that.

This leads to improvements in behavior as well. Edmister told me, "You're going to deal with that behavior on the front-end or the back-end...I'm a principal and I deal with no behavior issues." This stems from the emphasis the school puts on teaching *standards*-standards for learning and standards for behavior. They go hand in hand.

A fellow principal in my district, Heather Stewart, once likened standards-based instruction to driving a car. When adults get behind the wheel of a car, they have routines and processes in place to be successful. They check their surroundings, mirrors, and make sure their seat is comfortable and adjusted appropriately. After years of experience, they typically don't follow a checklist, and they can jump in and drive just about any car. A young person, however, has only the minimal skills to be successful in driving a car, and sometimes not even those. The inexperienced driver doesn't know to check blind spots and can't always figure out safe behavior.

One of the major questions we need to ask about standards-based instruction is: how much knowledge meets the standard? Do students need to be as experienced as 40-year-old drivers? Do students need to be novices, but know enough to be safe on the road? Or should they be somewhere in between?

Edmister has asked these types of questions and has found a way for his students to be successful. One aspect of this is allowing all teachers to provide evidence to aggregate the students' grades. Furthermore, having standards-based instruction allows teachers to identify and focus on the power standards that really matter to students. Despite years of experience and knowledge that "covering the content" is a horrible way to teach, we still do it every day in schools.

Homework

Imagine for a moment that your boss checks to make sure you are on-task throughout the day (micromanager, much?). When lunchtime comes around, you only get 30 minutes. You're not allowed to leave work at all during the day and rarely do you get breaks. And then, right as you are heading from one project to the next, he says, without much warning, "Oh, by the way, you have an hour of work that I need you to do tonight, and it is due tomorrow." You start to complain, but then realize it is fruitless, because not only can you not find a better job, but you also can't really be fired from this job. You're actually *required* to work here.

What would your satisfaction with your job be? How would you enjoy coming to work every day? This is what we do with our students. Of course, some schools are much worse than this, while others are much better.

You may feel like you're in a similar situation yourself. I'm not naive enough to think that educators don't go home and work in the evenings or at weekends. As an aside, let's ask why teachers put in so much extra work. Sure, there's not enough time in the day, but teachers also care very much about their work being successful with students. They put in the extra hours because they want to see powerful growth and development from their students.

Do teachers' students ever care about the coursework as much as teachers do? Not usually! We put so much effort into our work, only to have the kids blow it off at their first opportunity. How do we change what we are doing so that kids are actually enrolled in it? So that they want to be part of it even when they are not in school?

This may have been the original goal of homework: to engage kids in their learning. But it has greatly lost its flavor. In her book *How To Be a Happier Parent*,[30] KJ Dell'Antonia references homework in a negative way more than 200 times. And one whole chapter is devoted to how to make homework manageable. There are hundreds of other titles that talk negatively about homework. Isn't it appalling that our system has created such a poor experience for families? The "10-minute rule" is commonly cited in the US, whereby kids do 10 minutes of homework a night for each grade level. Under this rule, a second-grader should do no more than 20 minutes, yet we are still asking them to do so much more than that.

The author and leadership guru Joshua Spodek talks about experiential learning as a way to turn homework battles into a thing of the past. In our current system, he told me, the teacher takes care of everything. She goes on and on making, creating, organizing, figuring out, planning, assessing, and grading. Spodek asks us to do the opposite: to put the

---

30 KJ Dell'Antonia, *How To Be a Happier Parent*, Avery, 2018

planning, learning, and organizing in the hands of the kids. That's a big ask and it needs to happen incrementally. But a teacher can start handing little things over to the students today, and eventually work up to something amazing.

Social and emotional learning

Mike Anderson, an educational consultant based in New Hampshire, says that schools often see social and emotional learning as an aside. In a 2015 article for the ASCD's *Educational Leadership* magazine,[31] he wrote:

> *"Only a few decades ago, most people felt that social and emotional skills should be taught primarily at home. Today, the proliferation of character education, antibullying, and social skills programs signals a growing recognition of the important role of schools in promoting social and emotional learning, or SEL.*
>
> *Too often, however, schools teach social and emotional skills outside the daily curriculum. Consider how much more relevant such skills would be if we embedded them in daily work, supporting students as they learn to cooperate effectively with a lab partner, set realistic writing goals, persevere through a tough math problem, or self-regulate well enough to allow others to speak in a class discussion."*

When I talked to Anderson for the Transformative Leadership Summit: School Experience, he told me that we need to build SEL right into our learning, and that it is even identified clearly in the Common Core State Standards. He showed me how the skills required in the Common Core are the same skills needed to be successful with living!

Anderson offers three ways to make SEL a key part of our students' experience. First, he suggests identifying strategies for teaching those skills to kids. He invites us to review the standards we need to teach students, and look for the social and emotional skills that are embedded in the standards: self-awareness, self-management, social awareness, relationship

---

31 Mike Anderson, "Social-Emotional Learning and Academics: Better Together," *Educational Leadership*, 73:2, October 2015, tinyurl.com/y6vakhko

skills, responsible decision-making, overcoming peer pressure, and so on. By focusing on these skills in the planning stages, we can more effectively find ways to implement them in the day-to-day teaching.

Second, Anderson suggests sharing our power and control. This not only helps the kids, but it also relieves a great burden from us. I remember my first day as a principal. The assistant principal and the secretaries were in the office before school started, talking about some sort of parent communication, and they said, "What do you want to do with this?" I remember feeling shocked that a simple issue like this needed my input to happen. It was clear that the parents needed communication and any one of those people could have made that decision, but it fell to me. I gave my answer, but then realized that I should have given up that control. I should have asked, "What do you think needs to happen?" Instead, I created a system where they needed me to answer even the littlest questions. I didn't give up my power and control, and that required me to forever be the only one making decisions.

A few years later, and much wiser, I issued a challenge to students and staff that would require a monumental effort. I gave them seven school days to come up with a plan for a new initiative that would be student-driven. The teachers recognized that they couldn't give kids enough time to do the work needed, so they suggested that we cancel classes one day and focus on meeting that initiative. Because of my costly mistake on my first day as a principal, I knew better than to own every process. The teachers saw a need and organized an effort to make it happen.

Third, Anderson suggests that we give kids more choice. He says that adults tend to "swoop in and overmanage" situations; we need to let kids flounder and persevere a bit more. He told me, "If you're persevering, you've got your reason for doing it." If a student totally gives up, we can be pretty certain they don't have a reason for doing the work. It's not easy for adults to let kids have choice all the time, but taking a few steps in that direction will teach them way more than they can get out of a textbook.

PART 4
The parent and community experience

In education, you often hear teachers, board members, politicians, and others say that without us, kids and families would not know what to do.

Once, a teacher talked to me about students who have disabilities. She basically said that, for those students, school is the only place where they receive help or structure – their parents don't have an idea of how to help them. She didn't realize that my daughter has Down syndrome, and she was lumping my daughter in with this group of kids that would be lost if not for her and other educators like her. That rubbed me the wrong way.

On other occasions, when I've talked about home visits, people have said, "Oh, you want to visit their home so you can see how awful their life is and have more empathy?" No! I want to visit students' homes so they know that I care enough to leave my ivory tower.

Here are three things that can help you to overcome the savior complex.

1. Don't judge parents. Just stop it. Seriously.
2. Have positive intentions (H/T to the elementary principal and author Melinda Miller). Assume the best. Don't make up their story for them – learn from them and ask them what they are doing.
3. Recognize that people are doing the best they can. The number of parents who are actively hurting their kids is remarkably small. Are parents struggling because they don't have the skills, abilities, time, and

143

resources to be better? Yes! I sure am! I am a well-educated, successful white dude and I still struggle to be as good a dad as I can be.

The truth is, parents are awesome. Expectations and mindsets are powerful, and if we believe parents are doing the best they can, we will see evidence of that. Let's make sure the storyline is that parents are amazing and doing great things.

This is a tough issue to tackle, because teachers often think they are helping or being courageous, when all they are doing is distancing themselves from the very people with whom they should be partners. And maybe partners is not even the right word. Perhaps the correct word is supporters. In our current educational climate, there is more and more choice for parents on where and how their children are educated. Ultimately, it is the responsibility of the parent to educate their child and we are simply supporters of that goal. For example, I had a parent tell me she was going to home-school her daughter. She said she was worried I would be upset with her. I told her that she didn't need to worry and my job was to support her in educating her child. I said she could come by any time and ask for whatever help she needed. She was blown away.

Dr. Kashi Bazemore is a great example of a supporter to parents. She grew up in Bertie County, North Carolina, and worked hard in her education. Her mom, an educator, was very involved and did a lot to make sure that Bazemore had all she needed. Bazemore went on to earn a doctorate and become an educator herself. She opened a charter school, where she served her community with what they needed to support their children. She knew that many parents would not be able to provide their children with transportation to school, so, at great expense, Bazemore and her team organized buses for all their students. She saw the value in being a partner with parents; she took it a step further and found a way to truly support them.

The chief communicator

I was watching a movie with my wife and the characters kept talking, but not communicating. Despite their best (or worst) efforts, they didn't really tell each other what they were thinking. They kept lying to save face and didn't give all the information. My wife exasperatedly said, "If people just gave their perspective, none of this drama would happen!" She was right. The movie wouldn't have existed if everyone had just said what they were experiencing.

How often do we let things fester and bother until someone finally communicates clearly? So many of our problems come down to communication, or lack thereof. If we want to find success, we must focus on clearly communicating – the good things and the bad things.

Will Parker, author of the book *Principal Matters*,[32] says that you are the chief communicator for your school. Parker has a great story about creating the right mindset to communicate with parents. When he was a child, his dad would take him outside to look at the moon through a telescope. What his young mind didn't understand was that you can only ever see one side of the moon. But when astronauts visited the moon for the first time, they saw all around it. As leaders, we are like the astronauts: we have lots of information and can see much more of the moon, but we are often only allowed to show one side of it. Our job should be to show more than one side of the moon.

So, how can we engage with parents in a truly powerful way? What parents really want is to know what is going on with their child's learning and school. With all the social media technology available, there are many great ways to communicate this. Parker suggests that we put our message out so that people can find it wherever they are. He even suggests doing a weekly newsletter. He told me, "We want to have the last word each week on what is going on in our schools."

Engaging with parents is incredibly important. You must have their attention and ears in order to make sure that your school meets their needs. The challenging part is recognizing that you should get input from parents (and teachers and students) about *what* needs to be implemented, not *how* things need to be implemented. This is a delicate balance that is not always easy to maintain. Although we strive to be partners with parents, we have expertise and we need to be OK with stating as much. We understand what we are allowed and not allowed to do in schools, and we have research to support different implementations.

---

32 William D. Parker, *Principal Matters: the motivation, courage and action needed for school leadership*, CreateSpace, 2015

Parents need to be regularly consulted on the what and occasionally on the how. For example, when he was principal at Skiatook High School in Oklahoma, Parker knew that parents needed positive communication about the school. And he knew that he needed a multi-faceted approach to get that to them. So he used Facebook, Twitter, email newsletters, newspapers, and more to get that positive word out. He saw the need from the parents and he decided on the best way to make that happen.

Sometimes a parent will express that they need their child to learn a lesson. In fact, this just happened recently. A student engaged in some low-level poor behavior that was just high enough to warrant a phone call home. When I spoke to the student's mom, she said that her daughter needed something more than a lunch detention and that maybe she should pull her out of school for a couple of days to teach her a lesson. I told her that the lesson had been learned through a conversation with me.

In this situation, I knew that suspension was certainly not the right response, and that the student just needed some time to reset and process what she should have done instead. It was a simple solution. Mom wanted to come get her right then, but I assured her the lesson had been learned.

Even though we have the authority to determine the how, we should still seek parent input now and then. Districts and schools across the country work hard to find ways to engage parents in the conversation about strategic plans and goals, and those methods traditionally produce very poor results. A 10-15% response rate on a survey is pretty good! Excellent principals work hard to get as much information as possible from parents, by engaging with them through a variety of channels.

Strategies for communication
- Carry a device to capture moments.
- Distribute these through multiple platforms.
- Use Facebook to boost some posts.
- Send a weekly newsletter.
- Use your media relationships to your advantage.
- Make sure your community consistently hears about the positive things at your school.

A process for communication

Despite our best efforts to engage, support, and be there for parents, there is still a good chance that someone will get upset about something. When that happens, I have a process to work through.

1. What's the worst that can happen?
2. Listen and have integrity.
3. Ask what a resolution looks like for them.
4. Be clear about what you will do. Then do it!

To help explain this process, I'm going to share the story of a parent I worked with. This parent was actually a grandmother; she was raising her grandchildren because their mom was in jail and their dad was not allowed to visit them (at first). Grandma (we'll call her Lisa, because Grandma sounds too cuddly) was fairly young, but she had a lot of life experience. She was affiliated with a major Latino gang in Southern California. She was not ashamed of her past, nor was she proud of it, but she also wasn't quiet about it. She knew the world that her grandchildren were growing up in and she knew what they would be exposed to. One of Lisa's most frequent sayings was, "I'm raising these boys to be strong men who stand up for themselves and take care of their own problems." I'm sure you can imagine what that led to: lots of fighting and physically aggressive behavior, which meant that Lisa and I talked together a lot. It also meant that we didn't see eye to eye in most behavioral situations.

What's the worst that can happen?

We ask this question not so that we can be overwhelmed with worry, but so that we can put the situation in perspective. This is a valuable first step. We have to realize that parents being upset is not the end of the world. Usually, parents are upset because communication with them has failed somewhere along the way. That's too bad, but it is not the end of the world. Honestly, ask yourself what's the worst that can happen. If that parent is unstable, things could get physical or even dangerous, but that is rarely the outcome. Once you know what the worst thing that can happen is, you can approach the rest of this process appropriately.

With Lisa, the worst that could happen could have been pretty bad, but she was committed to changing her life and not being a "grandma gangbanger." She would say, "I've got to grow up and hopefully keep these boys out of prison!" When uncles or Grandpa came to pick the boys up, they could be scary and intimidating. Things were often tense for everyone when they were around. I knew that Lisa wouldn't ever do anything, but for me, the worst that could happen was that one of these uncles could be waiting for me after everybody else had left the building. I was acutely aware of that very slim possibility. Being aware of the potential fallout allowed me to be very intentional about #4 in the process, which we will get to.

You don't have bad parents in your school. You have people who are doing the best they possibly can with what they have. Sometimes, that leads to parents getting upset for seemingly no reason. As you go through this process, some questions will inevitably arise that will help you to look at the parent in a different light. What are some reasons why they are reacting the way they are? Could they be frustrated with their own parenting skills and looking for someone to blame? Could they think they could do your job so much better? Could they have other experiences that have prepared them for this moment, in positive or negative ways?

There are so many reasons why they could be acting the way they are. Once you ask yourself what's the worst that could happen, you will see that there are a lot of potential outcomes. The worst one is probably not very bad at all.

Listen and have integrity

This is the most important step. You must listen to what the parent is saying. You must hear them completely, ask questions to make sure you understand what is going on, and be aware of what they are trying to express.

This requires you to do all the important parts of active listening: sitting appropriately; maintaining appropriate eye contact; listening; rephrasing what they said; asking questions to elicit deeper answers; allowing pauses; maintaining a calm voice; not sharing what you shouldn't share.

When Lisa was upset, she would unload all kinds of complaints and problems. Her issues were so deep, there was no way in the world that we were going to address even a tenth of what she brought up. I listened, I stayed calm, and I asked questions about what was pertinent to me and the school. Her other issues weren't my business and they weren't germane to our issue at hand. At first, she would demand to know what was happening to the other students involved in the incident. I had various responses to this question:

- "I'm here to talk about your child, Lisa."
- "You wouldn't want me to talk about what is going on with your student, so I'm not going to answer any questions about someone else's student."
- "I understand your frustration and knowing about the other students isn't going to help you deal with your student."
- "How I deal with each student and their family is very much adapted to each student and their circumstances. That's why I'm taking the time with you right now. Let's talk about your student and use our time to support him."

Eventually, those questions stopped being a fishing expedition for her and we could get back on track with this statement: "Thank you for asking, Lisa. You know I'm not going to say anything at all about those other students."

Conversations with upset parents can be confrontational, but it is vital that you listen closely to identify what the issue actually is. One of the best ways to ensure that you understand is to rephrase. For example, "What I'm hearing you say is that this other student has been harassing your student for two weeks and today he finally had enough. Is that a fair summary?" Sometimes you get it wrong, so you keep rephrasing until the parent appears satisfied that you have heard them.

It might go without saying, but you can't get agitated yourself. Especially during the listening phase, you have got to keep your cool. Speak slower, speak softer. When you do this, it invites the other person to do the same. It's almost annoying to me how slow and soft my speech becomes when I have an upset parent. It seems so counterintuitive to get them to listen by being quiet, but it actually works.

One time, Lisa was with her husband and they were both yelling at me about how we weren't fair in suspending their grandson. I spoke so softly that they could see my mouth moving but couldn't hear what I was saying over their yelling. Almost instantly, they stopped and leaned in to hear. I was saying, "I wonder what he thinks about his consequence." Lisa and Grandpa were so fired up that they hadn't stopped to think about their student. I had already done the work with him to know that he was good with the consequence, so we asked him. Thank goodness, he said very clearly that he was OK with it.

When I say have integrity, it means that you do what is right, regardless of the circumstances. At one school, I had a very difficult situation that I handled exactly by the book, but it still didn't make people happy. Parents were upset. Kids were upset. Even though, technically, I had done nothing wrong. I needed to admit that I had made a mistake. Rather than complain about the situation and blame the policies that required me to act that way, I had to apologize for the way it was handled.

Ask what a resolution looks like for them

It is easy to forget this step, but it saves you so much time. Sometimes parents have a very clear idea of what it will take for them to be satisfied. It might be moving the student out of a teacher's classroom. It might be big changes to a longstanding policy. Depending on your situation, this may or may not be appropriate. Regardless of what you can or can't do, knowing what the parent actually wants makes it much easier to de-escalate the situation.

I worked with one parent who wanted the entire school to revolve around her daughter. She wanted absences removed, tardies eliminated, and all kinds of other things that just could not be accommodated. When it became clear that those were the only things that would satisfy her, I responded, "I can't change these things for you. I'm sorry that I won't be able to meet your desires."

When you understand what a resolution looks like for the parent, it is significantly easier to know when your conversation is actually completed. It seems like a no-brainer, but often we don't ask this question.

Another parent once came to me to raise a litany of complaints against her students' teachers. She had even printed out a list of all her concerns. Seeing that, I thought she would be satisfied only with blood! But when I asked her what a resolution looked like, her response floored me. She said, "I don't really need a resolution. If I don't get these things off my chest, I'm going to be frustrated for a very long time, and it's not worth it to me. I just need to know that you hear me." Wow! I sure was glad I asked, because that list had made me very nervous.

Through my conversations with Lisa, of which there were many, I realized that her idea of a resolution was that she could confirm that I had thoroughly investigated complaints, accusations, and incidents, and that I was treating her grandson fairly. She knew that people judged him because of his mom's past and her past. She didn't want that. Although she came to our conversations frustrated, upset, angry, and confused in the beginning, as I asked her each time what a good resolution looked like, she was able to articulate her desires more clearly. In a short time, a combative relationship turned into one of respect and appreciation on both sides.

Be clear about what you will do. Then do it!

Parents typically want to be heard and have good communication from the school. There's a recipe for making an upset parent even more upset: say one thing and do something different. Sometimes we don't do this intentionally, and as we gain more information, it can become challenging to stick to something we may have said too soon.

But if you say you're going to call, you'd better call. If you say you're going to implement a certain consequence, you had better do that, too.

One conversation with Lisa was especially rocky. Her grandson had done something that was worthy of suspension and I had told her that. I didn't want to suspend him, but it was pretty much out of my hands at that point. I told her that I would collect all the work from the teacher and have it ready when she picked him up during her lunch break. Well, guess what happened? I didn't do that, because of some other emergency, so when Lisa arrived, her grandson was ready to go, but he didn't have any work.

Lisa was rightfully upset. And she let me have it, too. Right in the front office. That situation and others like it helped me to see how vitally important it is to keep your word. I apologized and made other arrangements, so that she could get back to work and the student still had an opportunity to get some work done. It was not a fun experience and it sowed a seed of doubt about me in Lisa's mind. Thankfully, I learned from it. In the end, Lisa stopped being the "upset parent" and became a supportive, engaged partner with our school. She knew she didn't have to get fired up any more, because we had established what a resolution looked like and we could figure it out together.

Managing your school's social media

Many of the principals I talk to are concerned about how much time it can take to do the work of posting moments to social media. Managing multiple social media accounts can be a tricky (and possibly expensive) endeavor. It is therefore imperative that you find a way to make it easier on yourself.

You need an easy and intuitive way to interact with all your school's stakeholders. I have a fairly slick process that I use to post to all social media pages for my school (Instagram, Facebook, and Twitter). It goes something like this…

It all starts with Instagram

Instagram is the hardest platform to get information into. For some reason, you aren't permitted to post through anything other than the official app, which can makes it difficult and annoying to post. If anybody knows how I can improve this workflow, please let me know!

I start with Instagram because everyone loves pictures (and videos) and they get the most interaction. Whenever I want to share something with the community, it goes on Instagram, with the school hashtag somewhere in the text accompanying the picture (or video). I use a school-issued iPad with the Instagram app installed and signed into the school Instagram account.

This next part might be a little tricky to follow here in the book, but there is a blog post on my website that shows how to make it happen: tinyurl.com/yczoa4az

I set up "recipes" in IFTTT.com (If This Then That), which gets all your apps talking to each other. This makes it easy to post to all the other social media pages without any further interaction from me. I use a school account for IFTTT. Here is a handy flow chart to help make sense of it all.

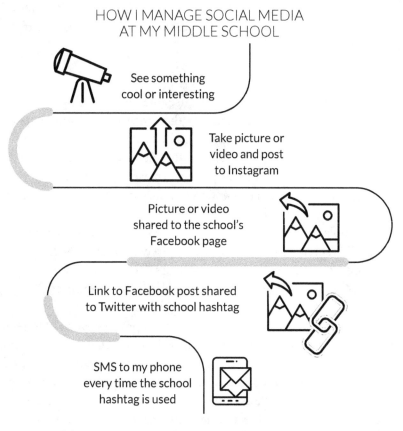

HOW I MANAGE SOCIAL MEDIA
AT MY MIDDLE SCHOOL

See something cool or interesting

Take picture or video and post to Instagram

Picture or video shared to the school's Facebook page

Link to Facebook post shared to Twitter with school hashtag

SMS to my phone every time the school hashtag is used

You can follow the recipes that I use, which are posted on my blog. Once you set everything up in IFTTT, then it is really easy to start using the recipes for yourself.

I have a recipe for videos posted to Instagram. IFTTT creates a link post on Facebook. After that link post arrives on Facebook, the second recipe posts it to Twitter. It also makes sure that the school hashtag shows up. My third recipe ensures that all photos on Instagram end up on Facebook, too. The next recipe takes any photos posted to Facebook and publishes them to Twitter as well. This will also post any other picture to Twitter, in case you post directly to Facebook instead of via Instagram. The fifth recipe just makes sure that all the admin posts to your Facebook page are sent out to Twitter, too.

I love this process because it makes it easy for an administrator to post just once a day to Instagram and get the word out on many different channels at once.

Empathy

In the software design world, they use the term "eating your own dogfood" or "dogfooding" to describe the process of gaining empathy. Dogfooding means that you actually use the tools that you are creating for other people. This term is especially apt when we talk about the parent experience. Much of the parent experience is hidden to us, as educators, because we don't interact with parents nearly as much as we interact with students and other teachers.

For example, in my schools, we have used PowerSchool for tracking grading. This software program has an entirely different look for parents than it does for teachers and administrators. There is a way to see what the parents see, but it is not very intuitive and it can be quite challenging to remember to look at what a parent might see.

In the empathy stage of the design-thinking process, we have to really work hard to know what parents are experiencing. One way that Acton Academy in Austin, Texas, does this is by surveying parents on a weekly basis. Jeff Sandefer, the co-founder of Acton Academy, comes from a business background, so he asks parents if they are pleased with the work of Acton and if they would recommend the school to their friends. These powerful questions enable the staff to see how well they are meeting the needs of parents. Sometimes there are complaints, but the constant feedback allows the school to move on quickly.

To gain empathy for what our parents experience, we really need to start by asking them. But one of the best ways that we can gain empathy *without* asking is by listening to the complaints that we receive. When parents take the time to complain, there are messages hidden within that we need to find. One year, I got a complaint about a particular teacher not responding to email. This teacher certainly struggled with this task, although I kept thinking it was not as big a deal as this one parent made it out to be. It turned out that this parent was the canary in the coal mine.

When I later asked for a Semester 1 commentary on our school's service, I received numerous anonymous complaints about our communication. This was disheartening, as I felt we were doing some really neat things that should have been shouted from the rooftops. I didn't listen as well as I should have when the parent brought her concern to me originally and I could have saved us some heartache.

For Dr. Kashi Bazemore, gaining empathy is easy, because she actively connects with everyone she can. I say easy, but it is really a monumental task for her to expend the effort it requires to communicate with so many people. Bazemore is part of the Chamber of Commerce, the Lions, the Rotary, and every other group she can possibly be a part of. She does all this to make sure that she is aware of the needs and concerns of her community. She constantly asks how people are experiencing her school and what their level of satisfaction is, although not always using those words.

Ask, ask, ask. Figure out what your parents are experiencing, find their pain points, and do something small to get started!

Prototype

I find that some parts of prototyping with parents take longer than we might expect to see results. This is natural, since we don't get feedback from parents all the time. It is important to keep going even when things are difficult. We may not see the fruits of our labor very quickly when it comes to parents. But we will get there!

Reflect

Earlier, Will Parker encouraged us to write a weekly email to parents about what we are doing in our schools. He suggests we have the final word on our school for each week – and we make it positive. I would encourage you to use a free tool, like Mailchimp, for this newsletter. Mailchimp will give you feedback about your emails that you can use when determining what you should continue doing.

Mailchimp shows you how many people opened your email and how many times parents clicked on a link in the email. Low numbers don't mean that your communication is good or bad, but they do mean that you can see what response you are getting from people. When I sent out an email on the last day of school before winter break, with a request for a survey response, I only had a couple of clicks to the survey. So, when we came back after the break, I sent the survey link again, which helped me to get a better response. In the end, about 10% of parents responded.

In all areas, seek feedback from parents, then reflect on how you can do your work better to meet their needs.

Iterate

You're not going to please every parent! Don't try to, but do try to improve the experience for them as much as you can.

One thing I ask parents is, "How would it be best to communicate with you?" They often say they don't know. I get it: they are busy, just like everyone else. What I want my parents to know is that I *do* want to communicate with them. My philosophy is that we need to be everywhere for them. Our job is to make it easy for them to find us.

Partnership with parents

In education, we are truly partners with parents if we are really doing a good job. Otherwise, we are simply supports for parents. Parents have the primary responsibility of raising, teaching, and training their children to be successful adults.

I hate to say it, but in many ways we have attempted to steal that authority from them. Although school breakfast, lunch, and, yes, even dinner programs seem like a good idea, in many ways we are taking away the awesome responsibility from parents and they are left with even less time to raise their students. I started this part of the book by talking about the savior complex that we have as educators. Parents will never be our partners if they feel that we are doing their job for them.

In order to be partners, a few things have to happen. We have to first recognize that parents are ultimately responsible for the success of their students. It is not enough for us to *pretend* deference to them. We need to actually ask them what qualities and skills they want in their students. We need to ask them how we can best serve them and help them to fulfill the dreams they have for their children.

Being partners is about sharing the load, but even in a law firm, there is a managing partner. That managing partner is the parent. Yes, we are experts in education. Yes, we have a lot of school experience. But we also need to see that the desires and needs of the parents are being met.

One of the ways that the educator Katie Kinnaman does this is by having office hours at Starbucks. She lets parents know that she will be there and will meet with anyone who needs to chat. Of course, a public place outside of school is not the place to have deep and personal discussions about students. But it is a place to talk about the vision of the school and how you are doing in meeting the needs of parents.

What the community experiences

It was front-page news in the small Kansas town, but it was also front-page news around the country. "A Newly-Hired Kansas Principal Resigned After Student Reporters Investigated Her Credentials"[33] was the headline for *Time* magazine. One article mentioned that the students went to their superintendent before they published the article, to ask him if they should publish it. Knowing the possible ramifications of students exposing *his* mistake, the superintendent still suggested that they go ahead.

As I read this story, I knew I had to connect with him. When Destry Brown answered the phone, he was still in a little shell shock from all the attention around this incident. I was amazed by what he told me: "I will sacrifice my discomfort for [the students] to have success." Not only was Brown willing to sacrifice himself, but he also wanted the students to have a real opportunity. As I talked with him more, I learned that although the story that made national news was the principal's resignation, there was so much more to it. Brown engaged the community in so much more than just a student newspaper. He went out of his way to establish relationships with community partners to give kids real opportunities in the workplace.

---

33 Katie Reilly, "A Newly-Hired Kansas Principal Resigned After Student Reporters Investigated her Credentials," *Time*, 2017, tinyurl.com/y7zgccxv

When we think of community engagement, we often have an ulterior motive: money. Fundraising, sponsorships, booster clubs, and similar activities are usually what we think of. But Brown found success in partnerships, where both the school district and the community are working toward the same goals.

Brown told me that it all started a few years earlier, when the district looked at its male Hispanic population and saw that many of them were dropping out of high school. The school added career pathways and invited the young men to take classes that would prepare them to make money much sooner. Brown told me, "When we added masonry and construction trades, it made them really engaged in school." These capable, intelligent young men were not engaged in school because school was not meeting their needs.

Adding these trades was an important step, but Brown knew that he couldn't do it alone. He worked with community businesses to help identify the skills they needed. This had a two-fold benefit. First, the community was interested and engaged in the educational program; they had a say and they had an opportunity to help design it. Second, the community knew that they would have graduates with specific skills who could do the work that was required.

With all the other things that need to be done in a school, it's no wonder that a principal doesn't spend much time thinking about how the community experiences the school. But, this is an important task, albeit a challenging one. I hope that you can take a few of these examples and find ways to engage just a little bit more with your community.

Meeting the community where they are

How do you start to garner community support for what you are doing? You need to have a vision as a leader. At this point in the book, I may be sounding like a broken record. When people know your vision, they can start to find their place in it.

When I was about 15, my dad said, "I sure hope my kids grow up to be better than me." I didn't understand then what I understand now. I thought, "My dad has been alive for a long time! Why in the world hasn't he figured it out yet? If he wants to be better, why isn't he just better?

Who would want their kids to be better than them? My dad's awesome!" What I know now, as a parent, is that I want my kids to be stronger and better than me. I want them to not be saddled with the weaknesses that I have. I want them to be able to overcome the challenges I faced and not be held back by them.

I'm not alone. Every parent wants what is best for their child. There is not a parent out there who wishes their child would have a mediocre education and grow up to be a bum. We hear time and time again from people in our communities that they want their kids to be able to have a better education than they did. Inherently, people know that education is a ticket out of a negative situation, and an enhancement of a good situation. So, when you have a vision, people in the community want to be part of it.

Glenn Robbins, the former superintendent of Tabernacle Township in New Jersey, says it is crucial to go out into the community to learn what others are doing. In Tabernacle, the mayor owned a large cranberry bog and Robbins was excited to engage him in teaching the students about how he managed such a large operation, especially using technology. With these connections and relationships, Robbins is able to go beyond just volunteering in the classroom. He finds people who are doing cool things and lets them share those cool things with his students.

It's much easier for the community to buy in to what you're doing at your school when they get to bring their passions to you. At my school, we had a parent who really wanted to do a pageant for her daughter's age group. She wanted to teach leadership skills and self-respect. As we opened our doors to her, she asked to get time off work to come to our school and build this pageant from the ground up.

Katie Kinnaman was a principal in Palo Alto, California, where there were many parents who were immigrants to the US. Kinnaman noticed that the only people who ever showed up to the meetings and information sessions at school were parents who could already speak English. Her student population suggested that there should be more Spanish-speaking parents at her meetings, but they rarely attended. Through her PTA, Kinnaman learned that a group of parents wanted to meet with her and she would be only English speaker at that meeting.

Her PTA president recommended that they meet off-campus and address the parents' issues. Kinnaman had a translator, but knew how challenging it was going to be for her to be in that environment and be able to understand so little. She understood that it was probably how so many parents often feel in our schools.

Well, she had the meeting with the parents and resolved their concerns. The community saw that she cared enough to be in their space, rather than only in her space. This was not an easy thing for her to do, but it was a powerful and simple solution to a complex problem. She went into the community and heard what people had to say.

Kinnaman also finds ways to meet parents and community members informally. You see, it's not all about having an event where you are the main attraction. If Kinnaman only stayed in her school and asked everyone to come to her, she would have never have an opportunity to build an actual relationship with her community members.

After all this effort, when Kinnaman needed something for school, who do you think was first to support her? The people with whom she had build that relationship of trust.

Community walks

Shane Safir, founding principal of June Jordan School for Equity in San Francisco, knew her staff needed to understand the community on a deeper level. So she adopted what she calls community walks. She worked hard to create an environment of learning and empathy for these walks, so that her staff would "primary-source data of their students' communities and experiences and stories to develop cultural proficiencies."

To be clear, Safir's work did not involve walking around and judging parents and families; it involved walking the community and understanding the journey the families had been on to arrive where they were. With more than 30 different languages spoken in the school community, there were bound to be great differences in how they perceived her and the school.

Community walks can work in any kind of school with many different cultures and with what we think of as a single community. They start with a student giving a presentation about a particular subgroup that he or she belongs to, telling the story of that subgroup. A powerful example that Shane mentioned to me is the unaccompanied minor group. These are students who have crossed the border into the US without having an adult with them. Their story can include being separated from family, sleeping on floors, and being alone for a long time.

The students tell their story, and then the student or another community member accompanies the small group of staff members on a walk through the community, sharing more about what they are seeing. The event ends in a family home, where staff can learn intimately about that family and hear their story of how they came to where they are now. And, of course, food is a universal language, so providing that is an especially helpful way to bring people together.

Here are the steps that Safir suggests you follow to create your own community walk.

1. **Identify subgroups to focus on**. You may have a very diverse school, or you may have a less diverse school, but there *is* diversity there. No two people are the same. Take some time to think about the focus of the walk. Ask yourself these questions: why are we choosing to do a community walk? What community group do we hope to learn more about?

2. **Give teachers choice in who they should focus on**. Some teachers may be very uncomfortable with this approach, so let them ease into it by learning about a group they are more comfortable with.

3. **Organize at least one PD session to develop background knowledge**. A focused PD session, especially one led by a member of the community group, can have a big impact. It's not designed to evoke pity or sympathy, but rather to help teachers gain empathy for a different situation than their own.

4. **Create norms around how to show respect in the community**. Offending someone as part of this walk would certainly be counterproductive, so take the time to talk with parents and community members about how to appropriately show respect. For example, in Alaska, everyone removes their shoes when they enter a home. It's a small thing, but everyone notices when it is not done.

5. **Have structure in the itinerary.** Remember to end walks in a home. The power of ending walks in a home is evident in the intimacy of a home environment. Home is where the most important learning takes place for every child. Home is where they learn how to act when they are most comfortable.

6. **Build in post-walk professional conversation.** Reflect with your staff about what has been learned. Ask: how does this impact us? Conversation is important after the fact. Continue to ask challenging questions. What is going to change in your school because of these community walks? Build in a significant debrief process so that your staff can walk away with some meaningful action steps.

Conclusion

A teacher once asked me why things change so much. "Why can't we just say we are good enough at X and not keep changing things?" she lamented. I asked her if she ever had the same class two years in a row. Of course she didn't. I asked her if her class ever changed throughout the year. She admitted that it did. I told her that, as educators, we are working with people, first and foremost, and people, thankfully, are constantly evolving and growing. Every situation impacts us and changes us. And so, as educators, we are constantly exposed to that change.

I took over a school once and while I was pushing for improvement, the staff pretty much saw that as change, rather than as a growth opportunity. As I took on my new principal role, a domino effect happened: the whole office staff turned over as well. People who had been at that school for years decided to move on. I encouraged the teachers and staff to embrace this complete turnover in the front office as a time to start anew, to define themselves and the school in whatever way they wanted. Rather than fear change, we should embrace it, prepare for it, and make it successful.

There is another aspect to change that is quite challenging for many educators. When asked to change, many educators feel that the request for change is a judgment. All too often, they feel hurt and offended that someone would ask them to change, as if asking for change meant that everything they had done before was complete trash and a waste of time. That is not the case. I asked Seth Godin what he thought about this line of thinking and how educators can overcome it. Here is his response:

"This is design thinking. And I think design thinking is incredibly important, and it comes down to this important question: there's work that I'm doing – what's it for? An educator who is trying to work with a class of kids. Why? What's it for? This hour I'm going to spend cleaning my inbox, or going to a meeting – why? What's it for? Is the answer to that question best met by the work I am going to do?

So, if I'm dealing with some teachers – hard-working teachers, teachers who have their heart in the right place, teachers who have shown up, shown up, shown up, who have shown up to do this generous work – I ask them: what is it for? Is it to have your students get a good grade on a standardized exam? Why? What's that for? Is it to get them into college? Why? What's that for? Is it to make their parents happy? To make the administrators happy? Is it to get through the day without someone throwing a chair through the window? These actions we're taking, sending the kid to the principal's office, giving the kid an A – what's it for?

If we can have a conversation about what it's for, if we can get aligned about what it's for, it is entirely likely that hard-working, insightful people will come to similar conclusions about what to do next. And that doesn't require admitting that the old work was bad. Or even acknowledging or deciding that it was bad. The old work might have been fine, but for a different 'What's it for?' If it turns out that the purpose of school in the 1960s and 1970s was to create compliant factory workers because we had a shortage of them, then yeah, that was the right work to do if that was what you wanted to get out of them. But, if what you want to do to go forward is to create autonomous, creative, dignified, independent, hard-working, generous, connected idea workers, then maybe, because the what's-it-for has changed, then maybe what we're going to do all day has changed."

Have you asked your community, "What's it for?" What would they say? What would you say? I'm reminded of a great video by the rapper

Prince Ea, where he asks what school is for. You have to watch it to really get what I'm talking about: youtu.be/_PsLRgEYf9E

Prince Ea starts out with: "What is school for? Feel free to call me slow, but I spent 16 years going to school and I still don't know." He is not alone. So, what is school for? Prince Ea argues that it is for teaching soft skills, in addition to some reading, writing, and arithmetic. He asks us to see kids for more than a score.

He talks about kids being afraid to raise their hands, for fear of being wrong. But I think the bigger issue is that being "smart" in school can be seen as a weakness. Kids don't want to appear smart, because then they are accused of being teachers' pets, or worse.

You see, we often don't teach social skills, resilience, or grit in schools. And while those things are becoming more popular in schools, we are typically delivering fake attempts at teaching them. We manufacture the learning, just like we manufacture every other type of learning.

Well, guess what? Life is hard enough. We don't need to manufacture resilience or grit. What we need to do is help kids learn from their everyday experiences.

CPSIA information can be obtained
at www.ICGtesting.com
Printed in the USA
JSHW040150310720
6912JS00003B/6

9 781913 622114